James Gowans

Edinburgh and its Neighbourhood in the Days of our Grandfathers

A Series of Illustrations of the More Remarkable Old and New Buildings, and

Picturesque Scenery of Edinburgh, as they Appeared about 1830

James Gowans

Edinburgh and its Neighbourhood in the Days of our Grandfathers
A Series of Illustrations of the More Remarkable Old and New Buildings, and Picturesque Scenery of Edinburgh, as they Appeared about 1830

ISBN/EAN: 9783337107260

Printed in Europe, USA, Canada, Australia, Japan

Cover: Foto ©ninafisch / pixelio.de

More available books at **www.hansebooks.com**

EDINBURGH

AND ITS NEIGHBOURHOOD

IN THE DAYS OF OUR GRANDFATHERS

A Series of Illustrations

OF THE

MORE REMARKABLE OLD AND NEW BUILDINGS, AND

PICTURESQUE SCENERY OF EDINBURGH

AS THEY APPEARED ABOUT 1850

With Historical and Descriptive Sketches

BY

JAMES GOWANS

WITH EIGHTY ILLUSTRATIONS

LONDON

JOHN C. NIMMO

14, KING WILLIAM STREET, STRAND, W.C.

1886

The Ballantyne Press
Ballantyne & Hanson
Edinburgh & London

Prefatory Note.

HERE is, perhaps, no city in Europe that offers to the lover of picturesque scenery and student of history, a more interesting series of subjects for the pencil than Edinburgh. It is not surprising, therefore, that it has attracted the attention of the artist in an eminent degree; and that, in addition to many separate prints, representing both its special and general features, several fairly comprehensive illustrated books on Edinburgh have been produced at various times. Shepherd's Views, which are reproduced in this work, were executed about the year 1830, and when engraved, were published in 1833, in a volume which is now much prized by book-collectors. Their reissue at the present time is due to their great merit as representations at once faithful and artistic of historical and other edifices, now swept away or modified in the course of changes and improvements which have greatly altered the features of "the grey metropolis of the north." Portions of the original descriptive matter relating to a few of the Views have been preserved in the present volume; but in most cases the early notices have been superseded by entirely fresh sketches.

The engravings here collected with the explanatory notes are so arranged and connected as to convey to the stranger the most vivid idea of the external characteristics of the Old and New Town of Edinburgh, and of its striking scenic environment. For the sake of connection, the plan has been adopted of using the same title as the heading of each article, or distinct subject, as is engraved underneath each view.

Mr. Thomas H. Shepherd appears to have supported the Suffolk Street Exhibition, and his speciality was landscape. He exhibited four works during 1831–32. Mr. John Britton, the antiquary, who had something to do with the previous publication of Shepherd's Views, dedicated the volume to Sir Walter Scott.

May 1886.

List of Engravings.

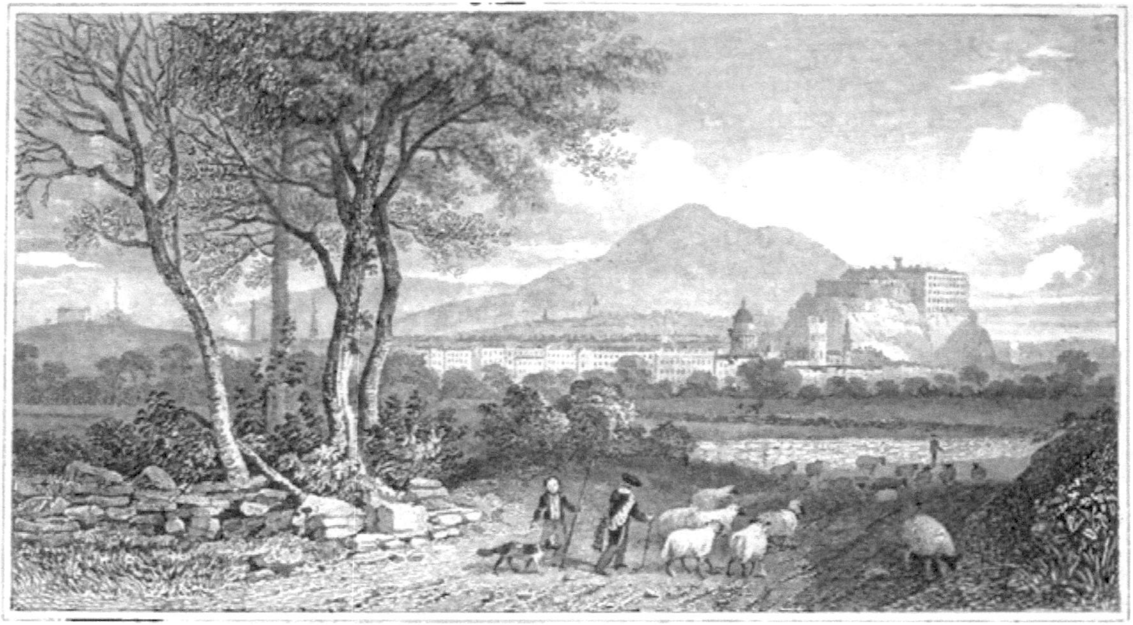

… by Th. H. Shepherd. Engraved by W. Tombleson

EDINBURGH

IN THE DAYS OF OUR GRANDFATHERS.

Edinburgh, from Craigleith.

T has been truly observed, that for situation and for the durability of its building materials, few cities have equal advantages to Edinburgh; and there is, perhaps, no town of which the general and distant effects are more striking and picturesque. The view before us, which represents the general aspect of the landscape and buildings to the north-west of Edinburgh as they appeared at the close of the reign of George IV., fully justifies this remark. In the distance, rising immediately above the Old Town, is seen the outline of a rocky eminence named Salisbury Crags, surmounted by the peak of Arthur's Seat. On the side of the city nearest the spectator is a level tract of rich land, which declines gradually to the Firth of Forth — now partially covered with handsome buildings. Occupying the apex of a peninsular rock are the varied buildings of the Castle, among which the factory-looking façade of the New Barracks constitutes a striking though not very appropriate feature. Immediately under the rock is the

A

spire of St. Cuthbert's and the tower of St. John's churches;
and near them the cupola of St. George's rises above the
buildings of the New Town by which it is surrounded.
Among the clustered rows of lofty houses in Edinburgh,
the prominent edifices are the churches of St. Giles and the
Tron, whilst to the left are seen the spire of St. Andrew's
Church and the monument erected to the memory of Lord
Melville. At the extremity of the print to the left are
shown, situated on the Calton Hill, a cenotaph column or
tower to the memory of Lord Nelson, and the fragment of
another building, called "The National Monument," designed
to commemorate all the soldiers and sailors who fell by land
and sea in the long war with France.

A little to the west of the point from which this view is
taken is Craigcrook Castle, a quaint old edifice, long the
residence of Lord Jeffrey. Gerald Massey, in his "Craigcrook Castle," thus finely describes this picturesque residence
and its surroundings:—

> " Mid glimpsing greenery at the hill-foot stands
> The castle with its tiny town of towers:
> A smiling martyr to the climbing strength
> Of ivy that will crown the old bald head,
> And roses that will mask him merry and young,
> Like an old man with children round his knees,
> With cups of colour reeling roses rise
> On walls and bushes, red and yellow and white;
> A dance and dazzle of roses range all round.
>
> The path runs down and peeps out in the lane
> That loiters on by fields of wheat and bean,
> Till the white-gleaming road winds cityward.
> Afar, in floods of sunshine blinding white,
> The city lieth in its quiet pride,
> With castled crown, looking on towns and shires,
> And hills from which cloud-highlands climb the heavens:
> A happy thing in glory smiles the Firth;
> Its flowing azure winding like an arm,
> Around the warm waist of the yielding land."

The Stone Quarries, Craigleith.

EDINBURGH, like Bath and a few other cities, is advantageously situated in regard to building materials. The excavations represented in the print, which are situated at the distance of about a mile and a half to the north-west of the New Town, supplied the greater portion of the stone with which that part of Edinburgh was built, and they are well worth the study of the geologist and of every stranger. The hill, at one end of which these excavations are made, is composed, almost to the surface, of freestone of a very white appearance and of solid texture. Here have been obtained blocks of immense size, which are susceptible of great delicacy of sculpture, as is exemplified in the capitals of the columns in Waterloo Place and in other parts of modern Edinburgh. The view of the city, seen in the distance, is similar to that already described as taken from Craigleith; the Castle rock, Arthur's Seat, and the Calton Hill being the most conspicuous objects.

The quarries here represented are not the only sources from which materials for the construction of the numerous public and private buildings which have recently been erected in and near Edinburgh have been obtained. Stones of various kinds and qualities, and adapted to particular uses, are to be found in almost every direction. The basaltic masses of Salisbury Crags and the adjacent heights at one time supplied durable materials for repairing the streets and highways of the Metropolis, and they also present numerous and varied specimens for the edification of the mineralogist and geologist. Objection, however, was taken to the mutilation of the Crags by the operations of the quarrymen, and the authorities wisely put a stop to the practice. In addition to the quarries of Redhall, Craigmillar, and Granton, another —situated at Hailes, three miles west of the Castle—gives freestone of a different quality from that of Craigleith. It consists of thin natural laminæ or layers, divided by a stratum of softer stone, and is chiefly used for pavement and the stairs of houses.

Possessing such advantages, both in the beauty of situation and in the stone obtained from the above-mentioned sources, Edinburgh has the means of vying in architectural embellishments with any other city in the United Kingdom. Much has already been done towards its improvement, and although the want of originality in some of the modern buildings detracts from their merit, others have been erected which do equal credit to the taste and sound judgment of the architects by whom they were designed.

To the south of Craigleith Quarry is the entrance to Ravelston, long the seat of a branch of the Foulis family, and more recently the residence of the Keith family, whose representative was Knight Marischal of Scotland. The quaint old mansion, surrounded by tall trees, still stands at the western extremity of the grounds, and it appears to have been erected in 1622. The Castle of Tully-veolan, with its terraced gardens, was evidently suggested to Sir Walter Scott by the house and gardens of Ravelston, although a representation of Craigcrook Castle is given for Tully-veolan in some of the editions of "Waverley." The gateway at the entrance to Tully-Veolan finds a counterpart in that at Traquair House, but the avenue, with its "broad continuous shade, through which Waverley approached the Highland Castle," has a remarkable resemblance to the avenue to Ravelston House, with which Sir Walter was quite familiar.

The Castle, from the Vennel.

THE Vennel is a steep and narrow street connecting the western extremity of the Grassmarket with the elevated ground formerly known as the High Riggs. To the south the view of the Castle from this position is peculiarly striking. The rock, as seen from it, is high and nearly perpendicular; and the ancient part of the fortress, rising from the very edge of the precipice, forms, as it were, an artificial and turreted prolongation of the rock itself. The modern buildings on the hill, known by the name of the New Barracks, are fortunately but little seen from this point of view.

By the abrupt termination of the High Street in the Castle rock, all accessible direct communication by it with the country and suburbs to the south was formerly entirely precluded. The new west approach has remedied this inconvenience. The foundation-stone of this structure was laid in the month of August 1827. A bottle of coins, the various newspapers of the day, and a plan of Edinburgh, were entombed on the occasion, with all the solemn ceremonies used and observed in like cases. The only open wall of the approach is a single arch, stretching from the Castle rock, in a south-westerly direction, to the high ground to the south, spanning the street which winds round the base of the rock, the situation in former days of the kings' stables, as shown by the name which part of it still retains, although no hoof of the royal stud has left an impression there for nearly three centuries. The communication between the arch and the Lawnmarket is formed by an elevated terrace, supported on the south by a strong inclined bulwark of stones. The approach to the centre of the old town by this road is

strikingly picturesque, the towering precipice, crowned by
the ancient walls of the Castle on the very extremity of its
jutting cliffs, being a boundary wall at once massive and
imposing.

The history of the fortress cannot be traced to its origin,
but recorded facts prove it to be of high antiquity. The
widow of Malcolm Canmore died here in 1093, a few days
after her husband was slain. The queen's body was conveyed through a now built-up postern gate on the western
side, and buried in Dunfermline Abbey, and her children
escaping at the same time, made their way to England to
their uncle, whilst Donald Bane, ignorant of this exit, was
besieging the opposite side of the Castle. It is mentioned
in a charter of David I. in 1128, and in 1174 it fell into the
hands of the English for the first time, as the price of the
liberation of King William I., surnamed The Lion, who had
been taken prisoner at Alnwick. On William's marriage
with the cousin of King Henry about twelve years afterwards, it was restored. The English held the Castle in the
time of Edward I., but it was recovered from them by
Randolph, the nephew of Robert Bruce, in 1313. During
this reign it was destroyed by Bruce to prevent the English
from taking possession of it. The Castle remained in this
ruined and desolate condition for twenty-four years. In
1336 it was rebuilt, and given up to Edward by Baliol,
but was soon afterwards taken from the English by Sir
William Ramsay. Falling again into their hands, it was
regained by Sir William Douglas. Chancellor Crichton, in
the reign of James II., shut himself up in it, and defied the
power of the King. In 1573 the brave Kirkaldy of Grange
held the Castle for thirty-three days against the united
efforts of the English and Scottish forces, till the mutiny
of his garrison obliged him to surrender.

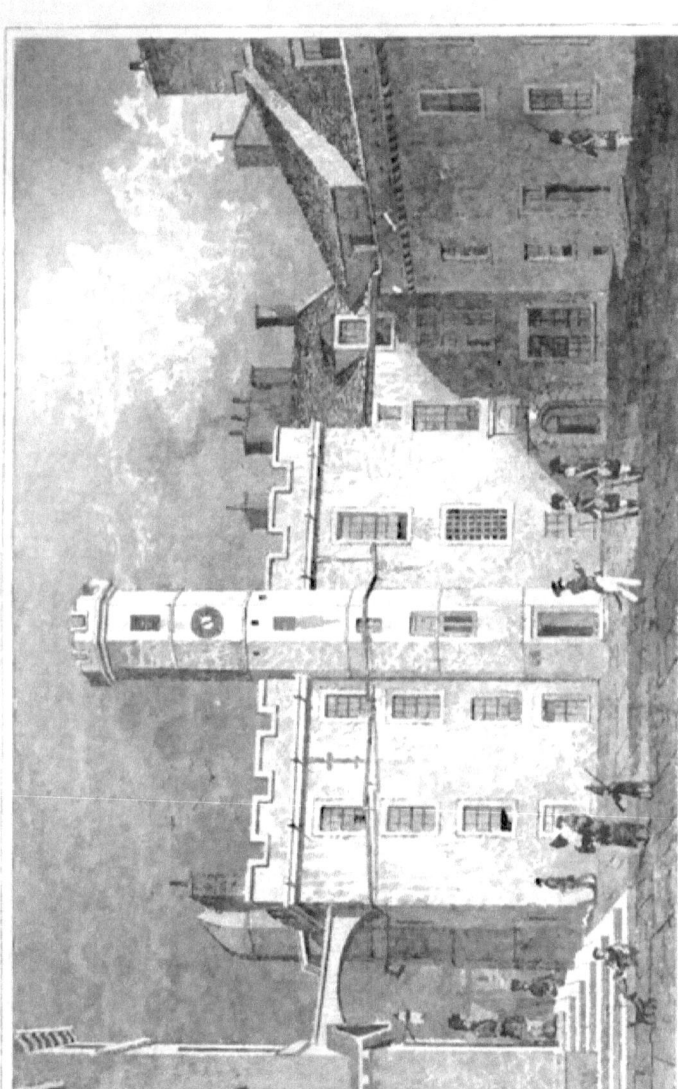

Drawn by Tho H. Shepherd

Engraved by J. Henshall

THE INTERIOR OF NEWGATE OR THE FELON'S GAOL.

The Interior Quadrangle of the Castle.

ENTERING the Castle from the Esplanade, the visitor, after passing a palisaded outer barrier, reaches a long vaulted archway, with traces of ancient portcullises and gates. Over this is the old state prison, where the Marquis of Argyle was confined before his execution.

Beyond this arch, on the right, is the Argyle Battery, and below it is Mylne's Battery, built in 1689. Further on are a bomb-proof powder magazine, the officers' quarters, the Ordnance Office, and the Armoury, capable of holding 30,000 muskets. The barracks can accommodate between 2000 and 3000 soldiers. On the south-west is Drury's Gun Battery, and on the summit is the King's Bastion, Mons Meg, and St. Margaret's Chapel, the latter of which has a special attraction from its being the oldest portion of the Castle, it having been erected towards the close of the eleventh century by Margaret, queen of Malcolm Canmore. This little chapel or oratory, which is in a fine state of preservation, measures about twenty-six feet by ten, and is probably the smallest ancient chapel in Scotland.

In the interior quadrangle of the Castle is an ancient building, which is rendered interesting by its history being most intimately connected with that of the country. The Parliament House was on the south side of the court, represented in the view, while the great state-rooms were on the side towards the city eastward.

From the appearance of the dates inscribed on the walls, these apartments were repaired at different times, up to the year 1616, although the general character of

the interior appears to support the theory that portions of
this building are older than any recorded dates.

In the year 1707 the regalia of Scotland were deposited
in a room in this part of the Castle, but having never
afterwards been exhibited, were reported to have been
secretly conveyed to London—a report generally believed
till the year 1818, when a Commission was appointed, of
which Sir Walter Scott was one, to examine the room
where they were supposed to be deposited. The Commission met at the house of the Governor on the 4th of
February, and accompanied by the military band and the
guard belonging to the Castle, opened the Royal Commission
and commenced their search. The outer door of the room,
which was of oak, was found strongly secured, and, when
forced open, discovered a second door, formed of gratings
of iron; and in the room beyond a large strong-box was
found, which contained the articles they were seeking.
They consisted of the royal crown, of pure gold, richly
ornamented with precious stones, the sceptre, and an
official rod of silver. The crown, at least the circlet, is
supposed to be as old as the time of Robert Bruce. It
was last used at the coronation of Charles II. before the
battle of Worcester. In the Crown Room are also deposited
four memorials of the House of Stuart, which belonged to
Cardinal York.

What is now a military hospital was formerly the
Parliament House, where banquets were frequently held
and state prisoners tried. The dimensions of the Great
Hall are roughly 80 in length by 33 in breadth,
with a height of about 27 feet. There is no record of
the time when the hall was altered and transformed into
a military hospital, but it is supposed to have been done
about the beginning of the present century.

The West Bow, from the Lawnmarket.

THE West Bow was originally a narrow crooked street, leading by a steep and difficult ascent from the Grassmarket to the Lawnmarket, which forms a continuation of the High Street westwards, and was at one time the only passage by which a cart or vehicle could enter that part of the city from the south. Commencing at the Grassmarket, the Bow followed the line of the lower portion of Victoria Street. It then abruptly struck northwards to the Lawnmarket, coming out opposite the house of Dr. Anderson, the celebrated pill-vendor. Until within the last few years, the east side of the upper portion remained in all its original and picturesque integrity, the corner house with its wooden front being specially admired. A few of the more recent of the old houses still stand at the south-west end of the Bow. Here were the mansion in which Provost Stewart entertained Prince Charles Edward, the old Assembly Rooms, and several houses built by the Knights-Templars. The Bow was formerly to a large extent inhabited by white-smiths, whose families were said to have been so accustomed to the clatter of hammers that they could not sleep on Sunday mornings for want of the usual accompaniment. One of these whitesmiths was William Mitchell, the so-called "Tinklerian Doctor," who is described by Sir Walter Scott as "a curious mixture of madness, knavery, absurdity, and something like humour." Mr. Charles Kirkpatrick Sharpe, in his introduction to Law's "Memorialls: or the Memorable Things that fell out Within this Island of Brittain from 1638 to 1684," gives an interesting account of the salient

characteristics of the curious pamphlets which Mitchell issued
from time to time to edify his fellow-citizens. Sharpe says
they are full of amusing nonsense, and were generally
adorned with a rude cut of the Mitchell arms. In one of
his tracts Mitchell gives a curious account of a visit he made
to France. He says, "Their women seem to be modest, for
they have no farding-gales. The greatest wonder I saw in
France was to see the bra' people sit down on their knees in
the clarty ground, when the priest comes by carrying the
cross, to give a sick person the sacrament."

In this street resided the notorious Major Weir, who is
generally believed to have been a consummate hypocrite. In
the seventeenth century his so-called diabolical orgies created
a great sensation. He was accused by his contemporaries of
unnatural crimes, and it was alleged that, by magical incan-
tations, he had intercourse with the nether world. It is
possible that the poor old Major was slightly insane, and
that under the cruelties inflicted upon him he confessed to
impossible offences. Be this as it may, the Major was tried
in Edinburgh in 1670, found guilty, and sentenced to be
strangled and burnt between Edinburgh and Leith. The
Major's sister, an undoubted lunatic, was also tried at the
same time and sentenced to be hanged in the Grassmarket.

After the death of the Major, a halo of superstition surrounded the house, and no one would occupy it as a dwelling.
Dr. Robert Chambers, in his "Traditions of Edinburgh," states
that at the beginning of this century the proprietor of the
house succeeded in obtaining as a tenant William Patullo, a
poor man of dissipated habits. He says Patullo and his wife
saw the apparition of a calf, and they left the house "next
morning; and for another half-century no other attempt was
made to embank this part of the world of light from the
aggressions of the world of darkness."

The Grassmarket, looking West.

THE Grassmarket is a spacious street, or rather oblong quadrangle of houses, lying immediately to the south of and overlooked by the Castle Hill. It is the western portion of the southern of the two deep valleys which diverge from the precipitous rock on which the Castle is built. These, after separating to a considerable distance, again gradually approach and ultimately reunite at the Palace of Holyrood —including between them the High Street and its numerous closes, which composed the whole of the more ancient part of the city.

The Grassmarket was known in former days by the rather unclassical appellation of "The Sheep Fechts." Its spacious area long afforded a market-place for corn and cattle. It has, however, been shorn of half its glories, the Cattle Market having been transferred to an enclosed area to the south-west of it. The Grassmarket, long celebrated as a place of bustle and of life, was, at no distant date, renowned also as a place of death. It was the chosen site of the gallows, the former locality of which is still marked out by a peculiar arrangement of the pavement at its eastern extremity. Here was the place of martyrdom. Here, too, was Captain Porteous sacrificed to the fury of an organised body of citizens in 1736—a circumstance which has led to the ample consecration, both of the street and the event, in the pages of "The Heart of Midlothian."

On the north the Grassmarket communicates with the road to the Castle Hill by a steep lane, bordered with houses, known as the Castle Wynd. Opposite to this wynd, on the south side of the Grassmarket, is a narrow and somewhat steep street, termed Heriot's Bridge, which gives entrance to the grounds and to the north gateway of Heriot's Hospital. This entrance was, in former times, reached by a structure known in the language of the day as a bridge, which took its rise from the very middle of the Grassmarket. But although the bridge be entirely gone, the name remains as the distinctive appellation of a street where no bridge is to be seen. The Corn Market in the days of Shepherd was situated at its western extremity, and was the only public edifice in the street, unless two " wells " for supplying the inhabitants with water could be regarded in that light. Referring to the general characteristics of the houses in the Grassmarket, Dr. Daniel Wilson says, " Several of the older houses are built with bartisaned roofs and ornamental copings, designed to afford their inmates an uninterrupted view of the magnificent pageants that were wont to defile through the wide area below, or of the gloomy tragedies that were so frequently enacted there between the Restoration and the Revolution. One of these, which stands immediately to the west of Heriot's Bridge, exhibits a very perfect specimen of the antique style of window. The folding shutters and transom of oak remain entire below, and the glass in the upper part is set in an ornamental pattern of lead. Still finer though less perfect specimens of the same early fashion remain in a tenement on the north side, bearing the date 1634. It forms the front building at the entrance to Plainstane's Close,—a distinctive title, implying its former respectability as a paved alley. A handsome projecting turnpike stair bears over its entrance the common inscription : BLISSET—BE—GOD—FOR—AL—HIS—GIFTIS, with the initials I. L. G. K. ; and the windows above retain the old oaken mullions and transoms, richly carved in a variety of patterns."

Engraved by W. Watkins

Heriot's Hospital, from the Castle Hill.

THIS beautiful structure stands on a rising ground immediately south of and overlooking the Grassmarket. George Heriot, the founder, was the son of a goldsmith in Edinburgh, and himself afterwards jeweller, first to the Queen of James VI., and thereafter to the King himself. As a citizen of Edinburgh, he seems to have been held in considerable esteem. The honours of Deacon of the Incorporation of Goldsmiths were more than once conferred upon him. On the accession of King James to the throne of England, Heriot moved to London, and there, under the patronage of his royal master, speedily realised a considerable fortune. In the year 1623 he made a settlement of his affairs, by which, after leaving a large number of legacies to his friends, and acquitting a number of his debtors of his claims against them, he bequeathed the free residue of his property to the magistrates and ministers of Edinburgh, for the endowment of an hospital for the " maintenance, relief, and bringing up" of poor and fatherless boys, the sons of burgesses of the city. Dr. Walter Balcanquall, Dean of Durham and Rochester, was appointed to see the settlement carried into effect.

Heriot died in 1624, and in 1628 the building of the Hospital was commenced. Its progress, however, was for some time interrupted by the civil war. After a considerable interval, operations were resumed upon it in 1642, and continued till 1650, when Cromwell took possession of it as an hospital for his sick and wounded soldiers. It continued to be thus occupied for about eight years, when General Monk, on the earnest request of the Governors,

agreed on certain conditions to evacuate it. In the year
1659 it was opened for the purpose of the Foundation, thirty
boys being then admitted into it. It was not, however,
until the year 1660 that the building was fully completed.
It was understood to have cost, in all, the sum of £27,000,
a fact which seems to have raised the indignation of Maitland, the historian of Edinburgh, in no ordinary degree.

The architect of the Hospital is generally supposed to
have been Inigo Jones, although the late Dr. John Hill Burton, in his " History of Scotland," states that it was designed
by William Aytoun. The Hospital has a large income,
which, until the recent alteration in the mode of working
this Foundation, was devoted to the education and maintenance of about two hundred boys in the Hospital, and the
support of about twenty day schools in different parts of
the city, where education was furnished gratuitously to
several thousand children of both sexes. Last year the
Hospital was combined with the Watt College, under a
scheme sanctioned by the Scottish Educational Commission,
whereby efficient provision is made for a comprehensive
scheme of technical education as well as the education of
the children of poor burgesses.

On Founder's Day, which is the first Monday of June,
the boys in the Hospital decorate with flowers the statue
of George Heriot, which stands over the gateway. Several
relics of the founder are preserved in the Hospital, including
his forge and bellows, with " a hollow stone, fitted with a
stone cover or lid, which had been used as a receptacle for
and a means of extinguishing the living embers of the
furnace upon closing the shop at night." George Heriot's
workshop, from which these relics were removed, was only
about seven feet square, and was situated at the south-west
corner of St. Giles' Church.

Cowgate, looking East.

THE Cowgate is a long narrow street, running in a parallel direction to the High Street. It extends from the Grassmarket in the west to the foot of the Pleasance in the east. Shepherd's view is taken from a point at the foot of the Candlemaker Row. We are informed by a writer of the sixteenth century that the nobility, the senators of the College of Justice, and persons of the first distinction then had their residence in the Cowgate. But the fatal overthrow on the field of Flodden, and the consternation with which it overwhelmed the citizens of Edinburgh, made those who had withdrawn beyond the Royalty extremely anxious to have the existing city wall extended to defend them from the incursions of the English. This wall, commencing at the north-east part of the rock on which the Castle stands, descended thence in an oblique direction to the West Port: it then ascended part of the ridge on the opposite side, and afterwards took an easterly direction to the Bristo and Potterrow Ports, continuing to the Pleasance. Its direction here was northerly as far as the Cowgate Port, and ascending St. Mary's Wynd, joined the Old Town Wall, somewhat southward of the Netherbow Port. The ground on which the buildings of the Old Infirmary and the University are erected, is included within the circuit of this wall, and remains of it are still to be seen in the Vennel, Bristo Port, Drummond Street, and the Pleasance. Two interesting portions of the wall are to be seen in the Vennel and Bristo Port at the back of Society. The latter is curiously pierced for windows and other openings, whilst the former shows one of the Flodden towers, which was preserved from

destruction by the zealous efforts of the late Dr. Patrick
Neil, after the Town Council of the day had doomed that
it should be removed. The buildings in the Cowgate are
lofty, though of less elevation than those of the High
Street. Up till a comparatively recent date the Cowgate
contained a large number of those quaint wooden-fronted
tenements once so common in Edinburgh. One of the
most characteristic of those structures was the house of
Andrew Symson the printer. one of a series of antique
edifices between the Horse and College Wynds, but now
removed. On the south side of the Cowgate is the
Tailors' Hall, now part of the premises of a brewery. This
hall was used in 1656 as the place of meeting of the commissioners appointed by Cromwell to administer the forfeited
estates, and here also theatrical entertainments were held
before the erection of Allan Ramsay's theatre in Carrubber's
Close and the theatre in the Canongate.

Near the west end of the Cowgate rises the quaint
battlemented steeple of the Magdalen Chapel, which dates
from about 1503. It has in its windows the oldest
specimens of stained glass in Scotland. The Chapel was
dedicated to St. Mary Magdalene, and was left by the
foundress to the Hammermen of Edinburgh, in whose
possession it remained until recent years, when it was sold
to the Protestant Institute. Here the first General Assembly
of the Church of Scotland was held in 1560, and eighteen
years later, in April 1578, was held the thirty-sixth meeting, of which Andrew Melville was Moderator. The table
that stands in front of the desk of the Chapel is still pointed
out as that on which the body of the Earl of Argyle was
placed after his execution in 1661, and where it lay until
removed to the family burial-place at Kilmun, the head,
however, being affixed to the Tolbooth.

16'

Bank of Scotland.

This building, as it appears in Shepherd's drawing, was designed by Mr. Richard Crighton in 1806, and was built at a cost of £75,000, chiefly from unclaimed money in the possession of the Bank. The south front presented an elegant appearance when seen from Bank Street. The situation is at the south end of the Mound, the dead wall, where the declivity is greatest, being covered by a stone screen, with a balustrade. The basement in front was rusticated, and a range of Corinthian pilasters decorated the second story. There were four projections to this front, and over the door, in the recess formed in the centre, was a Venetian window, ornamented with two Corinthian columns, surmounted by the arms of the Bank. About 1868 the directors gave orders for the alteration and enlargement of the Bank, in accordance with designs furnished by the late Mr. David Bryce, R.S.A. It now presents a lofty, broad arch-based rear front to Princes Street, and, standing free from the buildings near it, forms a conspicuous object in the landscape. The great old centre has been expanded by the addition of two wings, and the elegant dome is surmounted by a figure of Fame, 7 feet in height. The Bank of Scotland is the oldest in the northern part of the kingdom, having been incorporated by royal charter in 1695. The original capital was £1,200,000 Scots, or £100,000 sterling, and the business was carried on in small premises in Old Bank Close, Lawnmarket, for 111 years. In 1774 an Act of Parliament was obtained authorising the Bank to double the amount of its original stock. According to the latest statute obtained

D

by the Bank, the directors acquired power to issue a total sum of £4,500,000, but it has never been taken advantage of. At present the subscribed capital of the Bank is £1,875,000, of which £1,250,000 is paid up.

To the west of the Bank is the nine-story block of buildings known as James's Court, the main entrance to which is from a passage in the Lawnmarket. It was built in 1727, and was at one time a semi-aristocratic quarter of the city, numerous peers, judges, and clergymen having houses in the court. Here David Hume, the historian, resided between the years 1762 and 1771, and Boswell, the biographer of the great lexicographer, had a house in the court, in which he entertained Dr. Johnson when on the way to visit the Hebrides. Dr. Hill Burton, in his "Life of David Hume," thus describes this locality:—"Entering one of the doors opposite to the main entrance, the stranger is sometimes led by a friend, wishing to afford him an agreeable surprise, down flight after flight of the steps of a stone staircase, and when he imagines he is descending so far into the bowels of the earth, he emerges on the edge of a cheerful, crowded thoroughfare, connecting together the old and new town, the latter of which lies spread before him in a contrast to the gloom from which he has emerged. When he looks up to the building containing the *upright* street through which he has descended, he sees that vast pile of tall houses standing at the head of the Mound, which creates astonishment in every visitor of Edinburgh. This vast fabric is built on the declivity of a hill, and thus one entering on the level of the Lawnmarket is at the height of several stories from the ground on the side next the New Town."

The County Hall and Signet Library.

THE former of these buildings, in which are held the county meetings, stands at the western extremity of the Library rooms of the Writers to the Signet, and is nearly a copy of that fine specimen of antiquity, the temple of Erychtheus in the Acropolis of Athens. Sir William Rae was so impressed by a model of the original which he saw at Paris, that he recommended it urgently to the Commissioners; and Mr. Archibald Elliot, the architect, who, prior to this, had furnished a design in the Doric style, having examined the fragments among the Elgin marbles, proceeded to carry the object into effect: in which he strictly adhered to the proportions and such parts of the original temple as were consistent with a modern building intended for a wholly different purpose.

In front of the principal entrance to the building four large fluted Ionic columns support a pediment, and two similar ones ornament the north end, pointing to the Lawnmarket. The length of the eastern front is rather more than 102 feet, and the northern about 57. The principal floor of the interior contains two large halls and rooms for business purposes. The building was commenced in 1816, and completed in 1819, at a total expense of £15,000.

The Signet Library extends along the range of buildings forming the southern side of the square composed by the County Hall and St. Giles's Church. The upper room of the Library is decorated upon a scale of great magnificence; a beautiful staircase leads to a spacious lobby, which is hung with numerous portraits of distinguished lawyers. From this lobby the visitor enters a truly splendid apartment, 132 feet in length by 40 in width, the ceiling of which is elliptically arched, and supported by twenty-four fluted Corinthian columns. The books, which include many of great value and rarity, are ranged in presses between and behind the pillars. A gallery, at the height of 20 feet, extends along the whole room.

Near the top of Liberton's Wynd, immediately behind the County Hall, stood Johnnie Dowie's Tavern, which has been appropriately termed the *Mermaid* Tavern of Edinburgh. Here the wits and men of letters of the last century were wont to assemble, to imbibe the strong ale and more potent spirits supplied by Johnnie. Amongst those who frequented this famous hostel were Robert Fergusson the poet, Martin the celebrated portrait-painter, and his famous pupil Sir Henry Raeburn; David Herd the ballad collector, and George Paton the antiquary. Burns and several of his associates, including Nicol and Masterton, had numerous meetings in this tavern during the Ayrshire bard's first visit to Edinburgh. Until its demolition in 1834, to make room for the approach to George IV. Bridge, this tavern was one of the lions of the Old Town.

Opposite the front of the County Hall at the north-west corner of St. Giles's Church, was the old Tolbooth Prison, made famous in literature by the magic pen of Sir Walter Scott, who designated it "The Heart of Midlothian." Howard visited this prison in 1782, and again in 1787, and on the last occasion expressed strong dissatisfaction at the nature of the accommodation for the prisoners. It, however, remained the prison of Edinburgh until 1817, when it was razed to the ground, without any regret being expressed as to its demolition.

The Parliament House.

THE Parliament House is built on the site of the old collegiate buildings and a portion of the burial-ground which formerly surrounded the Church of St. Giles. It was finished in 1640, at an expense of £11,600, and it is generally supposed that the designs were supplied by Inigo Jones. The National Convention, for whose meetings it was intended, was first known by the appellation of "Parliament" in the reign of Robert 1. The name was imported from England during the Bruce and Baliol competition.

The drawing does not represent the Parliament House as it was when really occupied as such. The older structure has been veneered and faced up to suit the taste of modern times. The building occupies the west side of Parliament Square. As it now stands, the Parliament House is in the form of an oblong quadrant, with open arcades of plain Grecian architecture, surmounted by the figures of four sphinx. The only part of it which remains in its original condition is the Great Hall, in which, prior to the Union, the Scottish Parliament held its sittings. The hall is 120 feet long, by upwards of 40 in breadth. Its roof is of dark oak, arched somewhat after the style of Westminster Hall. The floor and side benches are of the same material. The great south window is filled with stained glass, and the design represents the institution of the Court of Session by James V. in 1532. The walls of the hall are covered with portraits of eminent lawyers, and there are also several statues, including one of Baron Dundas by Chantrey.

The Advocates' Library is one of the five libraries in

the country which are entitled to a copy of every work
registered at Stationers' Hall and published in the United
Kingdom. The Library was founded in 1680, by Sir
George Mackenzie of Rosehaugh, a distinguished member
of the Faculty of Advocates. It was originally located in
one of the flats of a high tenement in a close near the
Parliament House, and narrowly escaped destruction by a
fire which occurred in 1700. The Library was then removed
to the larger apartments under the Parliament House, the
use of which was obtained from the Town Council, who
then appear to have been the owners. The Faculty did
not then obtain the exclusive use of the whole premises, a
considerable portion being required for the custody of the
national records, which remained in this place until the
erection of the Register House, when they were removed.

Amongst the many treasures of the Library are some
objects of special interest. Here is preserved the original
MS. of "Waverley" in a glass case. This precious document was presented to the Faculty of Advocates in 1850
by Mr. James Hall, advocate. Amongst the other treasures
displayed for the inspection of visitors are a MS. Bible
of the twelfth century; a copy of Ged's edition of Sallust,
the first book ever printed from stereotype plates; numerous
ancient MSS.; the King's Confession, sometimes termed
the First Covenant; the copy of the National Covenant
signed in Greyfriars' Churchyard in 1638; and several
state papers and letters of great importance, including four
letters of James V. to his Queen, fourteen letters of Queen
Mary written to her mother from France, and a letter from
the Duke of York (afterwards James II. of England) to his
father Charles I. The Library is estimated to contain about
400,000 volumes.

St. Giles's Church, County Hall, and Lawnmarket.

FOR continued bustle and business, for the number and diversity of its public and private buildings, the street or open area here represented is at once remarkably picturesque and interesting. About sixty years ago it was almost constantly occupied by dealers and chapmen, with bales of goods exposed for sale, exhibiting an ever-moving, ever-varying scene. Being a general mart for all kinds of mercery, it was inhabited mostly by tradesmen occupied in this business, and was the resort of retail dealers and private purchasers from all parts of the country. As represented in the annexed engraving, the webs of cloth and other goods were often displayed on open stalls in the middle of the street, and it thus assumed the appearance of a fair. This part of Edinburgh is familiarly known as the Lawnmarket. The principal object in the view is St. Giles's Church, which occupies the site of an older edifice, probably erected about the ninth century. A new church was erected in 1120 by Alexander I. The late Dr. W. Chambers, in his " History of St. Giles's Cathedral Church," says : " It consisted of a choir and nave, with small side aisles and central tower, built in a massive style of the early Norman period. From all that can be learned, it covered less space than is occupied by the present edifice. To this St. Giles's Church there are various references in old charters and other records. It is mentioned in an Act of the reign of Robert the Bruce. The circumstance of the Castle of Edinburgh having been selected as a residence by David I. is understood to have furthered the endowment and decora-

tion of St. Giles's. Various additions were made to the
Church from time to time, but in 1385, when Richard
II. invaded Scotland, he committed Edinburgh to the
flames, when the Church was virtually destroyed, the only
portions left being the entrance porch, a portion of the
choir and nave, and the portions that formed the base of
the spire." Two years later the reconstruction of the
Church was commenced, and it is generally supposed to
have been completed early in the fifteenth century. Dr.
Laing, in his introduction to " The Charters of the Collegiate
Church of St. Giles, Edinburgh," issued by the Bannatyne
Club, gives a minute account of the Preston Aisle, which
was erected by the Magistrates of Edinburgh to the memory
of William Preston of Gorton, who bequeathed to the Church
the arm-bone of St. Giles, which was then considered a
very valuable donation. In 1466, in virtue of a charter
of James III., the parish church of St. Giles was converted
into a collegiate foundation, with a chapter consisting of
a provost, curate, sixteen prebendaries, a minister of the
choir, four choristers, a sacristan, and a beadle, in addition to whom were the chaplains ministering at thirty-six
altars. Gawin Douglas the poet, and translator of Virgil's
Æneid, was Provost of the foundation before he was
appointed Bishop of Dunkeld. Consequent upon the progress of the Reformation in Scotland, the thirty-six altars
in the Church were removed, the effigy of the saint destroyed, and the fragments thrown into the Nor' Loch, and
the arm-bone of St. Giles, after being stripped of its precious
mountings, was cast forth as rubbish. The pillaged and
naked Church was the scene of the ministrations of John
Knox. " At that period there were no fixed pews. The
seats were chairs or wooden stools, provided chiefly by
worshippers for their own accommodation. The bulk of

the people stood, and they would gladly stand for hours listening to their favourite preacher." In 1572 the tower of the Church was fortified, and a military force was placed there by Kirkaldy of Grange, in the interest of Queen Mary, to overawe the citizens of Edinburgh. In 1603 James VI. bid farewell to the citizens of Edinburgh in this Church, on the eve of departing to ascend the throne of England. Notwithstanding his promise to uphold the faith of the Presbyterians, he established Episcopacy, and gave legal status to the Episcopalian order in 1612. Charles I., when he came to Scotland in 1633 to be crowned, re-established the Bishopric of Edinburgh, and St. Giles's Church was appointed the cathedral of the diocese. In July 1637 occurred the celebrated incident when a cutty stool is said to have been flung at the head of Dean Hannay when reading the new liturgy in St. Giles's, by "the half-mythical, half-historical Jenny Geddes." Episcopacy was subverted in 1639, to be again established in 1661.

In the course of the eighteenth century, by the erection of tasteless division walls, there were no fewer than four congregations accommodated within the walls of St. Giles'. These were the Choir or High Church in the east, the Tolbooth in the south-west, the Old Church in the middle and part of the south side, and the Little Kirk or Haddo's Hole in the north-west. In addition to these appropriations, the Preston Aisle was used as a place for meetings, and the dark central space under the spire, with the north transept, was used as the Police Office until the beginning of the present century. Clustering around the Church in the space now enclosed by railings were a series of little booths or shops, called "Krames," which were not removed until the year 1817, when the "Krames" were demolished. The external walls of the Church had a somewhat rough

appearance, which led to the inauguration of a movement for
the improvement of its exterior. At length a plan, prepared
by Mr. Burn, was sanctioned by the Town Council, and he
was instructed to carry it out. He commenced the alterations in 1829, and finished them in 1833. Experts and
lovers of old architecture unite in lamenting the bad taste
of Burn, whose renovations effectually destroyed the characteristic external features of the Church. Referring to this
blundering, Dr. William Chambers says:—"Burn changed
the entire exterior aspect of St. Giles's, the spire alone
excepted. Picturesque roofs and pinnacles disappeared.
The whole fabric was new cased in a bald style of art.
As concerns the interior, the sectioning into parts was only
modified. We are certainly left to lament that, from what-
ever cause, he took away or mutilated much that can never
be replaced."

An interior renovation of the Church was recently completed, under the superintendence of Messrs. Hay & Henderson, architects, whereby the beautiful features of the
pillars, walls, and roof have been made visible. For this
great work the public are chiefly indebted to the late Dr.
William Chambers, who contributed the larger part of the
funds. The Church, or Cathedral, as some prefer to call
it, is now one great expanse, without divisions. On the
walls of the Church are suspended a large number of the
old colours of the Scottish regiments, coloured engravings of
which, accompanied by historical notices of the regiments
they formerly belonged to, are given in Mr. Andrew Ross's
valuable work on " Old Scottish Regimental Colours."

Interior of the Signet Library.

THIS splendid Library Hall is enriched by paintings executed by Thomas Stothard, R.A., in 1822. Mr. Balfour Paul, advocate, describing the hall in his little work on "The Parliament House," says, "In the centre of the friezes opposite the entrance are represented Apollo and the Muses. Facing them, in three compartments, are portraits of orators, poets, historians and philosophers, placed as follows:—Immediately opposite the figure of Apollo is that of Demosthenes, on whose right is Cicero, and on his left Herodotus and Livy. To the left of these are historians and philosophers, the former being represented by Hume, Robertson, and Gibbon, and the latter by Sir Isaac Newton, Lord Bacon, Napier of Merchiston, and Adam Smith. In the group which contains the poets, Homer occupies the centre; on his right are Shakespeare and Burns, and on his left Milton and Virgil." This hall belonged at one time to the Faculty of Advocates, but they sold it to the Writers to the Signet about sixty years ago, not foreseeing that it would have been of the greatest advantage to them in future years, for the storage of a portion of their large and ever-increasing collection of books. The Library of the Writers to the Signet contains about 60,000 volumes, and is particularly rich in works treating of Scottish history and antiquities. The librarian for a lengthened period was Dr. David Laing, the distinguished antiquary, and one of the greatest bibliographers of the century. Laing was trained as a bookseller, and he carried on business for many years in partnership with his father. The versatile author of "Peter's Letters to his

Kinsfolk" thus describes the establishment of the Laings:
"As for shops of old books, classics, black-letter, foreign
literature, and the like, I never was in a great town which
possesses so few of them as this. There is, however, one
shop of this sort which might cut a very respectable figure
even in places where attainments are more in request. It
is situated, as it ought to be, in the immediate vicinity of the
College, and consequently quite out of the way of all
fashionable promenades and lounges; but, indeed, for anything that I have seen, it is not much frequented by young
gentlemen of the University. The daily visitors of Mr.
Laing seem rather to be a few scattered individuals of
various classes and professions, among whom, in spite of the
prevailing spirit and customs of the place, some love of
classical learning is still found to linger—retired clergymen
and the like, who make no great noise in the world, and,
indeed, are scarcely known to exist by the most part even
of the literary people of Edinburgh. The shop, notwithstanding, is a remarkably neat and comfortable one, and even
a lady might lounge in it without having her eye offended
or her gown soiled. Mr. Laing himself is a quiet, sedate-
looking old gentleman, who, although he has contrived to
make himself very rich in his business, has still the air of
being somewhat dissatisfied that so much more attention
should be paid by his fellow-citizens to the flimsy novels of
the day than to the solid and substantial articles which his
magazine displays. But his son is the chief enthusiast—
indeed, he is by far the most genuine specimen of the true
old-fashioned bibliopole that I ever saw exhibited in the
person of a young man. David Laing is still a very young
man, but Wastle tells me that he possesses a truly remarkable
degree of skill and knowledge in almost all departments of
bibliography."

E. Sargent   Square of S. Lucey

Part of the Old Town, from Princes Street.

THIS engraving represents one of the picturesque views which are commanded from the terrace of Princes Street, and also serves to show the remarkable arrangement and loftiness of the houses of the Old Town. Some of these houses consist of several floors, or flats as they are termed. From the inequality of surface on which these dwellings are raised, great variety of outline has resulted. The base of one mass is often on a level with the chimneys of another, and thus, whilst some families are living apparently in the clouds, others are doomed to dwell beneath the surface of the earth. In the foreground of the print is a clustered group of houses on the site now occupied by the Waverley Market and Canal Street. Above and beyond them is the North Bridge, and in the valley, now occupied by the North British Railway, were the public slaughter-houses. Rising from the valley, the houses are irregularly although closely planted on the side and summit of the ridge, and above them is seen the spire of the Tron Church. Immediately beyond the buildings to the east is displayed the abrupt and precipitous face of Salisbury Crags, which forms a sort of amphitheatrical wall of rock. Between the Crags and Arthur's Seat is a narrow valley or gorge called the Hunters' Bog, from the north end of which is obtained a fine view of the Firth of Forth and the interesting country on the opposite coast. From the summit the view is still more extensive, diversified, and impressive, as portions of twelve counties may be descried in the panorama it commands. As these rocks form conspicuous features in the scenery of Edinburgh and its vicinity,

and have supplied data for numerous geological disserta-
tions on their origin and structure, it may be interesting to
note that Maitland, one of the earliest historians of Edinburgh, conjectures that *Arthur's Seat* is a corruption of the
Gaelic *Ard-na-said*, "the height of arrows;" and "no spot of
ground," says Maitland, "is fitter for the exercise of archery
than this." Mr. Hugo Arnot, advocate, another historian of
Edinburgh, is of opinion that it obtained its name from
Prince Arthur, who in the sixth century defeated the Saxons
in this neighbourhood. Be this as it may, it is, however,
generally believed that Salisbury Crags are so called from
the Earl of Salisbury, who attended Edward III. in an expe-
dition against Scotland, and encamped on the slope behind
the rocky front. The path round the base of the Crags was
in former days a favourite walk of David Hume, Sir Walter
Scott, and Thomas Campbell. Scott, writing of this locality,
says: "If I were to choose a spot from which the rising or
setting sun could be seen to the greatest possible advantage,
it would be that wild path winding round the foot of the
high belt of semicircular rocks called Salisbury Crags, and
marking the verge of the steep descent which slopes down
into the glen on the south-eastern side of Edinburgh. The
prospect in its general outline commands a close-built high-
piled city, stretching itself out beneath in a form, which to a
romantic imagination may be supposed to represent that of a
dragon; now a noble arm of the sea, with its rocks, isles,
distant shores, and boundary of mountains; and now a fine
and fertile champaign country varied with hill and dale."

It is worthy of note, in connection with Arthur's Seat, that
there still lingers here a survival of the paganism of our forefathers, in the declining custom of young persons ascending
Arthur's Seat before sunrise on the first of May to gather dew.

Part of the Old Town.

(*Continued.*)

THIS scene is taken nearly from the same station as the former—that looking to the left hand, this to the right —and thus, when joined together, forming one continued view. Both serve to exhibit the peculiarity of the buildings and situation of Old Edinburgh, and also to show the hollow which separates it from the New Town. In one of the stately tenements here represented, there are no fewer than ten stories or flats, and it is a fact that many of these flats are inhabited by distinct families, whilst one flight of stairs gives access to the whole. Thus occupied, and thus constructed, it is not surprising that cleanliness was neglected, and that many slovenly and even filthy habits and customs ensued. In former days these stairs were only occasionally swept, and more rarely washed, and all kinds of domestic slops and offensive filth were thrown from the windows into the streets and closes. It was the custom, before emptying the contents of a vessel, for the housewife or servant to give the cry of "Gardeloo," and woe betide the casual passer by, if he did not understand the warning, as the contents might drop on his head, and if he escaped the full discharge, it might only be to secure a too ample supply of the loathsome liquid in the form of "jaups" or "splairges." Formerly the dangers from this practice caused English travellers to avoid Edinburgh; but, thanks to the general belief in the necessity of a practical application of the principles of sanitary science, the city is now one of the

cleanest in the country, and, as a corollary, the death-rate is
remarkably low.

Dr. Marwick, in his " History of the High Constables of
Edinburgh," states that at one time part of their duty was
to see after the cleansing of the streets, and it is recorded
that James VI. complained of the filthy condition of the
streets in the neighbourhood of Holyrood, which he said were
offensive to his royal visitors. At one time there were refuse
heaps at the foot of stairs, and in the corners of courts, and
much garbage was deposited on the streets. Sir James
Dick of Prestonfield, when Lord Provost of the city, caused
the streets to be cleansed, and the matter carted to his own
land in the neighbourhood of Duddingston, whereby it was
made very fertile. It was also the custom to empty "muck"
into the North Loch, and at the other side of the town it
was thought sufficient to simply convey the refuse to the city
gates. Pigs were kept in cellars, and even in dwelling-
houses, and Dr. Guthrie tells a story of finding a huge porker
in one of the upper flats of a house in the Cowgate, and
innocently asking how it had been got up, he was informed
that it had never been down.

In the annexed view the back of the Royal Exchange
forms a conspicuous feature at the left hand. The number
of windows gives it a sort of hospital or barrack appearance.
It is mostly used for the business of the Town Council
and Magistracy. This building will be described in a
subsequent page, to accompany a view representing its
chief front. Near the bottom of the print, at the edge of
the hollow, stood a building used as a sessional school, but
now removed, to the right of which is the Bank of Scotland.
The tower of St. Giles's Church is seen beyond the ridge of
houses, whilst part of the site of the old loch is also shown.

The Royal Exchange.

THE Royal Exchange is situated on the north side of the High Street, nearly opposite to St. Giles's Church, and is remarkable as being the first, or among the very earliest, of the modern buildings of Edinburgh. Early in the year 1753 the Town Council sanctioned the purchase of the decayed old houses which formerly stood on the site of this edifice, and in the same year the foundation-stone was laid; but the contract not having been finally settled, the building was not commenced until 1754. It was completed in 1761, at an expense of £31,500.

The Exchange is an elegant quadrangular building, enclosing a spacious open court, its northern side rising to the height of 100 feet; in length it is 111, and in breadth 57 feet. Pillars and arches forming a piazza support a platform with balustrades on the south front, facing the court, and four Corinthian pillars rising from this platform sustain a pediment, on which are the arms of the city of Edinburgh. Two wings extend southward from the ends of this side of the building, which are carried forward 131 feet, and, measured from the outer front of the northern portion of the building, will amount to 182 feet from north to south. A light colonnade forms the line of the southern side, above which is a platform with pilasters and vases. The entry to the court is under the colonnade through the central arch; all the other arches being built up, and the enclosed spaces occupied as shops. The court surrounded by these buildings measures 96 feet from north to south, including the piazza, and 86 from east to west. It is somewhat remarkable that

C

although the north front is hewn of stone, of more than 100 feet square, there is not a rent or crack perceivable in any part of it.

An endeavour was some time since made to induce the farmers, merchants, and others who were wont to assemble on the street to transact business, to remove their place of meeting to the more convenient and appropriate station of the court of the Exchange, but the attempt was unsuccessful. In the Council Chamber is a mysterious bronze statue, which, although shown as that of George III., is generally believed to be a representation of Prince Charles Edward. It is supposed to have been cast in France, as it was shipped at Dunkirk for Leith. While being unloaded the statue fell into the harbour, where it remained for some time. It was subsequently fished up, and after remaining at Leith for some years it found its way to Edinburgh, and after another rest was finally placed in the Council Chamber.

Opposite the entrance to the Royal Exchange there stood, until the year 1756, the ancient city cross of Edinburgh, a handsome octagonal structure, surmounted by a long shaft bearing the Scottish unicorn. It was removed by the Magistrates on the frivolous ground that it obstructed the thoroughfare, and the materials were dispersed, the shaft finding its way to Drum House, near Gilmerton. Last year a " Mercat Cross " in the style of the old cross was erected in the High Street, a little to the south-west of the old site, at the expense of Mr. Gladstone, which, on its completion, he handed over to the Lord Provost and Magistrates as representing the citizens of Edinburgh, when in Mid-Lothian on one of his political campaigns. The design for the cross was supplied by Mr. Sydney Mitchell, architect, and he is generally acknowledged to have been very successful in representing the characteristic features of " Dun-Edin's Cross."

House of John Knox.

On the north side of the High Street, near where the Netherbow Port or entrance to the city from the east formerly stood, is the manse or house of John Knox, the Scottish Reformer. The building is a plain, irregular-shaped edifice, with a wooden front and an external staircase. A pulpit ornaments one of the corners, and the occupant is generally supposed to have been Knox, but a minute study of the figure and its surroundings shows that it represents Moses receiving the law on Mount Sinai, the Deity being represented by a golden disc, with the name of God represented in three languages:

OEOS

DEUS

GOD.

On the outside, just above the lintel of the shop on the ground-floor, is the following inscription in an old style of lettering:

LVFE · GOD · ABVFE · AL · AND · YI · NYCHTBVE · [AS·] YI · SELF·

The word "as," after being obliterated, was restored during the renovation of the house. The words are the well-known scriptural command: "Love God above all, and thy neighbour as thyself." The house is divided into several small apartments, and it is questionable whether Knox occupied the whole building. Dr. Thomas M'Crie, the biographer of Knox, states that one evening in the spring of 1571 "a musket-ball was fired in at his window, and lodged in the roof of the apartment in which he was sitting.

It happened that he sat at the time in a different part of the room from that which he had been accustomed to occupy, otherwise the ball, from the direction it took, must have struck him." This incident favours the supposition that Knox resided in the first flat of the house. On this point Dr. Robert Chambers says: "The second floor is too high to have admitted of a musket being fired in at one of the windows. A ball fired in at the ground floor would not have struck the ceiling. The only feasible supposition in the case is that the Reformer dwelt in the *first floor*, which was not beyond an assassin's arm, and yet at such a height that a ball fired from the street would hit the ceiling." On the first floor is the study built for Knox in 1571 by the Magistrates of Edinburgh. when they ordered the Dean of Guild " with al diligence to mak ane warme studye of dailles [wainscot] to the minister Johne Knox, within his hous. above the hall of the same, with lyht and wyndokis thereunto, and all uther necessaris." In this house in 1559 Knox took up his abode along with his first wife, Marjorie Bowes, whom he had married while in exile. She, however, died shortly afterwards, and four years later Knox brought home his second wife. Margaret Stewart. youngest daughter of Lord Ochiltree. Knox's enemies did not hesitate to affirm that he had secured the affection of this lady by means of sorcery. In this quaint old mansion Knox held many conferences with the noblemen who favoured the Reformation, including the Earls of Murray, Morton, and Glencairn, Lords Boyd, Ruthven, Lindsay, and Ochiltree. Knox died in this house shortly after preaching in St. Giles's Church for the last time—on the 24th November 1572, and was buried in the churchyard to the south of the church, where a brass tablet marks the spot which tradition assigns as having been the grave of the Reformer.

36'

St. Mary's Wynd.

St. Mary's Wynd, so called from a religious house dedicated to that saint, was in the days of Shepherd a narrow lane of communication between the Canongate and the Cowgate. It still serves this purpose, but under the recent Improvement Act it has been greatly widened, the eastern side being entirely removed, along with Boyd's Close, wherein was situated the famous "White Horse Inn," in which, in 1773, Dr. Samuel Johnson put up. There is an Edinburgh tradition that Boyd, the landlord, was a keen patron of the turf, and having been successful in winning a coveted race with a white horse which he had trained, in remembrance of the profitable event he termed his place of entertainment "The White Horse," at the same time affixing an appropriate sign at the top of the outside stair which gave admission to the building. Between thirty and forty years ago the inn was the residence of a dairyman, who kept his cows in the dingy stables used by Boyd for the accommodation of his own horses and those of his guests. The religious buildings already referred to included a chapel dedicated to St. Mary, in connection with which there was an hospital for infirm persons. The income of the hospital appears to have been limited, for in 1550 the Town Council ordered all alms, oblations, &c., to be applied to the relief of the beadswomen by whom it was inhabited, and further ordained that each of the better class of citizens should make a day's visitation through the town to collect alms for the hospital, under a penalty of forty shillings. No trace of this building now remains.

This wynd in recent years attained a kind of notoriety

from being the recognised locality for the sale and exchange
of old apparel of all kinds, and the sale of new and inferior
ready-made garments. Traces of the old trade linger in the
street, as a few shop-fronts may still be seen covered with
old garments; and a scrutinising observer may occasionally
find a ticket in a window with the words, "Mournings lent
on hire." Robert Fergusson, in his poem on "Auld Reekie,"
thus refers to the associations of the locality :—

> " Now gin a loun should hae his claes
> In threadbare autumn o' their days,
> St. Mary, brokers' guardian saint,
> Will satisfy ilk ail and want,
> For many a hungry writer there
> Dives down at night in cleding bare ;
> And quickly rises to the view
> A gentleman, perfyte and new."

Previous to the commencement of the seventeenth century, owing to the high price of building ground, and the
habit which the inhabitants of Edinburgh had acquired of
living above each other in separate floors of the same house,
it had been necessary to raise the buildings to a very
dangerous height; it was therefore enacted by the Scottish
Parliament in 1698 that no new house facing a public street
should exceed five stories; but as this law applied only to
the front of a building, it not unfrequently happened that,
from the inequality of ground, the back part consists of
eight, ten, or even more floors. As many of the dwellings
in St. Mary's Wynd were considerably above the prescribed
standard and others below it, their disproportionate elevation,
coupled with the singularity of their projecting roofs and
embattled gables, gave a truly picturesque character to the
street, although the effect was much diminished by its
squalid appearance.

Drawn by Tho. J. Mulvaney.   Engraved by James B. Allen.

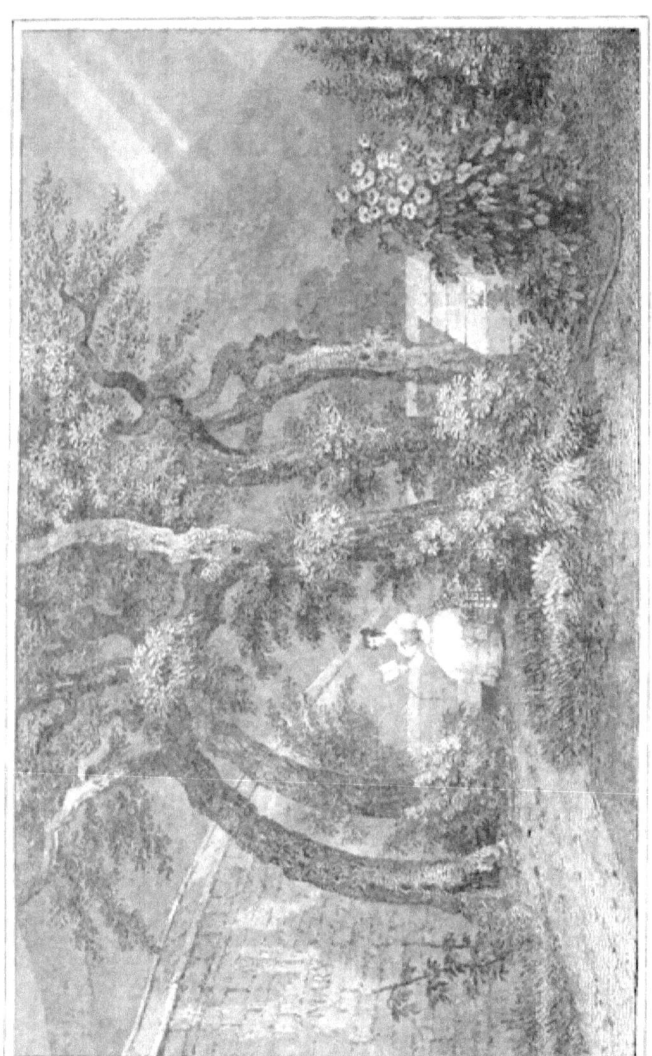

Moray House, Garden, &c.

On the south side of the Canongate, a little above the Church, stands the ancient mansion of Moray House, erected in 1628, by Mary, Countess of Home, a member of the Dudley family. Upon her death in 1645, the house passed into the hands of her daughter, Margaret, Countess of Moray. It thus became the property of the Moray family, and remained in their possession about two centuries. The entail was broken by a clause in one of the Acts of Parliament obtained by the North British Railway, by which they acquired this house, with a view to fit it up as a substitute for the Trinity Hospital which they had purchased. This arrangement was not, however, carried into effect. The House, which is occupied as a training-school by the Free Church, is still a conspicuous object, with its spacious entrance, its dome-roofed rooms covered with bas-reliefs, and its strong massive stone balcony overlooking the street. In 1648, when Cromwell came to Edinburgh after defeating the Duke of Hamilton in the north of England, he took up his quarters in Moray House, and again in 1650 he resided within this "solid spacious mansion," as Carlyle terms it. There is a statement in some of the old chronicles to the effect that during his first residence in Moray House Cromwell and his friends came to the conclusion "that there was a necessitie to take away the King's life." Be this as it may, there can be no doubt that within these old walls many schemes were planned which had important bearings upon the future history of Scotland. Within Moray House, in 1650, there took place the marriage of

Lord Lorne, the eldest son of the Marquis of Argyle, and
Lady Mary Stuart, eldest daughter of the Earl of Moray.
During the marriage festivities, the gallant Marquis of
Montrose, then a captive, was brought up the Canongate
past Moray House on a low cart attended by the common
executioner. The marriage party came out on the balcony
to witness the procession, and tradition states that one of the
Argyle family spat on the unfortunate Montrose, who gave
an indignant glance at the occupants of the balcony. Two
days afterwards. Montrose perished on the scaffold, but
within twelve years the Marquis of Argyle met his doom at
the hands of the public executioner in the streets of Edinburgh. In 1685, Lord Lorne, his successor, met a similar
fate, for having taken part in an insurrection in Scotland
against James II. When in Edinburgh, in 1881, the present
Marquis of Lorne and H.R.H. the Marchioness of Lorne,
were conducted by Dr. William Fraser to the historic balcony, from whence they viewed the scene of the memorable
episode in the career of Montrose, which has been so frequently sketched by Scottish artists.

At the period of the Treaty of Union, Moray House was
the residence of Chancellor Seafield, one of the statesmen
who negotiated the Treaty, and it is said that most of the
preliminaries of that intrigue were planned within its walls.
The remains of the picturesque old summer-house wherein
the Commissioners were scared by the excited populace
while signing the Treaty, still stand in the grounds attached
to Moray House, but the magnificent thorn tree which
adorned the upper terrace of the grounds, as well as the
curious arbour formed of the interlacing stems of trees, have
been swept away within living memory. The pleasant tradition that the thorn tree was planted by Queen Mary, and that

she was in the habit of using the arbour as a place for contemplation, cannot, unfortunately, be upheld, as there is undoubted evidence that the house was not then erected. The once current belief that Moray House was the residence of Regent Murray is equally destitute of foundation.

The stately terrace gardens behind were a place of resort and promenade at the close of the seventeenth century and the whole of the past, and it may be observed that the houses on the east side of St. John Street had doors opening into the grounds. They are now built up, but traces of them still remain. In the character of a lounging-place, the gardens are introduced in a scene in a play called "The Assembly," written in 1692 by Dr. Archibald Pitcairn. The comedy is thus summarised by Dr. Robert Chambers:—

"Will—'a discreet smart gentleman,' as he is termed in the prefixed list of *dramatis personæ*, but in reality a perfect debauchee—first makes an appointment with Violetta, his mistress, to meet her in this place; and as she is under the charge of a sourly-devout aunt, he has to propound the matter in metaphorical language. Pretending to expound a particular passage in the Song of Solomon, for the benefit of the dame, he thus gives the hint to her young *protégée*:—

"*Will.* 'Come, my beloved, let us walk in the fields, let us lodge in the villages.' The same metaphor still. The kirk, not having the liberty of bringing her servant to her mother's house, resolveth to meet him in the villages, such as the Canongate, in respect of Edinburgh; and the vineyard, such as my *Lady Murray's Yards*, to use a homely comparison.

"*Old Lady.* A wondrous young man this!

"*Will.* The eighth chapter towards the close: 'Thou that dwellest in the gardens, cause me to hear thy voice.'

"*Violetta.* That's still alluding to the metaphor of a gallant, who, by signs, warns his mistress to make haste—a whistle or so. The same, with early in the former chapter; that is to say, to-morrow by six o'clock. Make haste to accomplish our loves.

"*Old L.* Thou art a hopeful girl; I hope God has blest my pains on thee.

"In terms of this curious assignation, the third act opens in a walk in Lady Murray's Yards, when Will meets his beloved Violetta. After a great deal of badinage, in the style of Dryden's Comedies, which were probably Dr. Pitcairn's favourite models, the dialogue proceeds in the following style:—

"*Will.* I'll marry you at the rights, if you can find in your heart to give yourself to an honest fellow of no great fortune.

"*Vio.* In truth, sir, methinks it were fully as much for my future comfort to bestow myself, and any little fortune I have, upon you, as some reverend spark in a band and short cloak, with the patrimony of a good gift of prayer, and as little sense as his father, who was hanged in the Grassmarket for murdering the King's officers, had of honesty.

"*Will.* Then I must acknowledge, my dear madam, I am most damnably in love with you, and must have you by foul or fair means; choose you whether.

"*Vio.* I'll give you fair play in an honest way.

"*Will.* Then, madam, I can command a parson when I please; and if you be half so kind as I could wish, we'll take a hackney, and trot up to some curate's house; besides, a guinea or so will be charity to him, perhaps.

"*Vio.* Hold a little; I am hardly ready for that yet," &c.

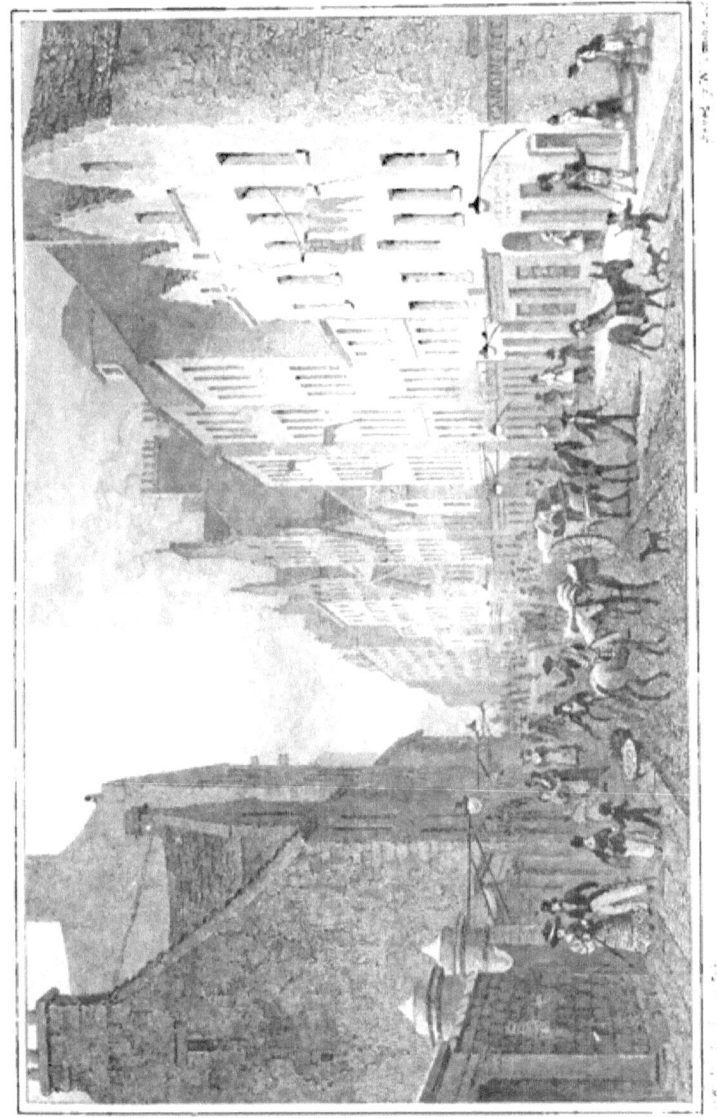

The Canongate, looking West.

With the exception of the Castle and the Palace of Holy-rood, there is, perhaps, no portion of the City of Edinburgh more interesting to the historical student than that termed the Canongate. Its origin is carried back by record to 1128, when King David I., who had recently endowed the Church of Holyrood, granted to the canons of that house permission to erect a burgh between their church and the burgh of Edinburgh, which at that time did not extend further east than the Nether Bow. In this burgh of Canongate the retainers and visitors of the monks of Holyrood were lodged and entertained for centuries,—here, in after ages, the ambassadors and envoys to the Court of Edinburgh took up their abode—and these very houses, in times comparatively modern, were the town residences and hotels of the nobility of Scotland, and formed, in fact, the court end of the city. The Canongate comprehends within its limits most of the eastern portion of Old Edinburgh, and had formerly a separate jurisdiction, with magistrates appointed by the Canons of Holyrood, to whom its inhabitants were subject, and to which church, until the erection of the present church in 1688, they mostly resorted, the service being Catholic, Presbyterian, or Episcopalian, at different periods. This district was, down to 1856, a Burgh of Barony, and was governed by a baron-bailie annually appointed by the Town Council of Edinburgh, who was assisted by other two bailies, termed resident bailies, elected by the ratepayers of the burgh. These bailies had the power of holding courts, and of deciding petty causes. The magistrates also held courts for the service of heirs.

Those inquiries were of a somewhat farcical character, as the bailies, along with a jury of shopkeepers and tradesmen, simply heard *ex parte* statements and made orders accordingly. The proceedings were recorded in the books of the court, and a certified extract issued from the Chancery Office constituted the title of the claimant or heir. The facility with which forged documents could be submitted and accepted as evidence was illustrated in the Stirling Peerage case, when the notorious Alexander Humphreys or Alexander claimed to be served heir of William, first Earl of Stirling. The bailies held the claim to have been duly established, and following up their decision. Humphreys attended at Holyrood in 1831 and 1835, and voted at the elections of Representative Peers for Scotland. In 1838 he was examined as to how he became possessed of the documents on which he founded his claim to the title of Earl of Stirling, and the answers not being satisfactory, the service was set aside by the peerage authorities. The following year Humphreys was tried for forgery before the High Court of Justiciary, when the jury returned a verdict of not proven.

Amongst the eminent men who resided in the Canongate about a century ago were numerous Scottish peers, judges, baronets, military and naval officers, and several distinguished men of letters, including Adam Smith, Dugald Stewart, Dr. Gregory, and Lords Monboddo and Kames. Gay, the author of "The Beggar's Opera," accompanied his patroness, the Duchess of Queensberry, to Scotland, and for some time acted as her private secretary. He resided in Queensberry House, and there is a local tradition that the poet regularly frequented a humble change house opposite the mansion of the Duchess, where he met the wits of Edinburgh.

The Canongate Church.

THE Parish Church of the Canongate was erected in 1688, but it has no architectural features worthy of note. Prior to that date the parishioners had worshipped in the Abbey of Holyrood, which at the Reformation was declared to be the parish church of Canongate. On the restoration of Holyrood Palace in 1659, after it had been almost entirely destroyed by fire, the private chapel was removed. This gave the advisers of the King an opportunity for suggesting that the parishioners should be deprived of the use of the Abbey Chapel as their parish church. In 1672 the Privy Council passed an Act declaring the Abbey Church to be "his Majesty's chapel in all time coming." It was not, however, until 1687 that the congregation had actually to remove. In that year James II. of England gave orders that the Abbey Church was to be fitted up as "our own Catholic chapel, and capable of the ceremonials and solemnities of the most ancient and most noble Order of the Thistle," and considerable sums were spent in supplying the necessary fittings. The homeless congregation found accommodation in Lady Yester's Church until the Canongate Church was erected. Dr. Hugh Blair, the author of the once-famous sermons, and the writer of "A Critical Essay on the Poems of Ossian," in which he defended their authenticity, was for some time a minister of this church, and, nearer our own time, Dr. John Lee, the "Archdeacon Meadow" of Hill Burton's "Book Hunter," was one of the ministers. The "Archdeacon," though he had an immense library, was frequently in the habit of visiting friends to ask the loan of a particular book, and his excuse for doing so was that, although he had several copies of the work, he could not lay his hands on one of them.

The churchyard contains a number of monuments erected to the memory of individuals of note, including Dugald Stewart, the metaphysician; Adam Smith, author of "The Wealth of Nations;" Bishop Keith, the historian of the Episcopal Church of Scotland; George Chalmers, who left his money for the establishment of an hospital for the sick and hurt; and Sir William Fettes, who bequeathed his estate for the endowment of a college for the education of the children of his less fortunate fellow-countrymen. In this churchyard also is the monument erected in 1787 by the poet Burns to the memory of his brother bard, the ill-starred Robert Fergusson.

On the one side is the following :—

HERE LIES
ROBERT FERGUSSON, Poet.
Born September 5, 1751.
Died October 16, 1774.

" No sculptured marble here—no pompous lay ;
No storied urn, or animated bust !
This simple stone directs pale Scotia's way
To pour her sorrows o'er her poet's dust."

The other side of the stone has the following words :—

By special grant of the Managers
To Robert Burns, who erected this stone,
This burial-ground is to remain sacred
To the memory of
ROBERT FERGUSSON.

About six years ago, Mr. William Ford, of the Holyrood Glass Works, erected in the churchyard a handsome monument of pale red granite : " In memory of the soldiers who died in Edinburgh Castle, situated in the parish of Canongate, interred here from the year 1692 to 1880."

THE CANONGATE TOLBOOTH

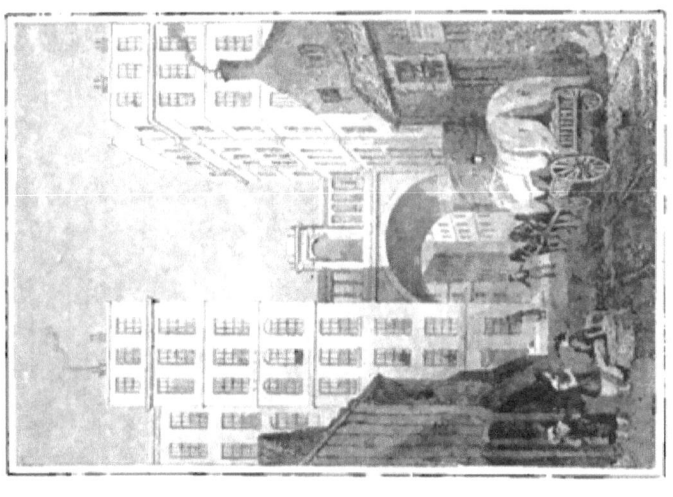

THE REGENT BRIDGE

The Canongate Tolbooth.

THE Tolbooth is a massive structure with corbelled turrets, built in 1591, in place of a previous one which stood on the same site. Like many prisons of a more recent date, the Tolbooth was evidently not intended to promote the comfort of the persons immured within its walls, as the apartments were both dark and small. The door of the old prison, which is several inches in thickness, is still to be seen closely studded with nails. The Tolbooth in bygone days was frequently tenanted by those who were persecuted in the cause of religious liberty, but more recently it was used as a prison for civil debtors. As the back windows of the prison are above the lane termed the Tolbooth Wynd, it was quite common for prisoners to be supplied with Lochrin or Sunbury whisky by their friends, who, when a string was let down from the rooms above, attached thereto bottles containing the much-coveted stimulant. On the archway at the top of the wynd may be read the inscription, "Patria et Posteris, 1591;" and the window immediately above is surmounted by a shield with a stag's head and cross, the arms of the ancient burgh. On the south front, between the windows of the hall, is a pediment surmounted by the national emblem—the thistle. The clock-tower contains two bells—one of them, of considerable antiquity, having the following inscription on its surface: "Soli Deo honor et gloria, 1608."

In the eastern portion of the building is the hall or court-room in which the bailies sat when considering the affairs of the burgh or dispensing justice. Of late years the

interior of the building has been considerably altered to
adapt it for a lecture-hall and reading-room, in which a
literary institute is at present domiciled.   The library of
the institution is shelved in one of the rooms of the adjacent
Tolbooth.

Immediately opposite the council chambers is Huntly
House, which was at one time the town residence of the
Gordon family.   This mansion was erected in 1570, and
is a characteristic specimen of the early domestic architecture of Scotland.   It presents to the street three timber-
fronted gables, rising from a series of quaint corbels, and the
cornice near the base is studded with sculptured tablets
filled with mottoes.   The westmost has "a device emblematic
of the resurrection, several stalks of wheat being represented
as growing out of bones," and the motto engraven, "Spes
Altera Vitae"—(there is hope of another life).   The original
entrance to the house was from the close behind.   In 1753,
when Maitland wrote his "History of Edinburgh," this house
was occupied by the distinguished Dowager-Duchess of
Gordon, the house of the Duke of Gordon at that time being
near the Castle.

In the Bakehouse Close, behind Huntly House, an ornamental arch gives access to the court in front of a house
erected in 1633, by Sir Archibald Acheson of Glencairney,
one of the Secretaries of State for Scotland.   The mansion is
a fine specimen of the domestic architecture of the period.
It is built of dressed stone, with sculptured dormer windows,
and string courses.   Over the moulded doorway is the
family crest—a cock standing on a trumpet, with the motto
"Vigilantibus."   The Earls of Gosford, the descendants of
Sir Charles, bear the same crest and motto.

The Regent Bridge.

In this print there is a view of the Regent Bridge taken from a point to the south in a street or thoroughfare bounded on both sides by old houses, in the now forgotten burgh of Calton. By the erection of Waterloo Place and the Regent Bridge, and the operations of the North British Railway, almost the whole of the houses of the old burgh have been swept away. The Regent Bridge was built at great expense in 1817-19. The arch over the Low Calton is 50 feet in width, with a height of 50 feet at the north end and 59 at the south, the difference being caused by the inequality of the ground. The depth of the arch is 82 feet. The street of the burgh was called St. Ninian's Row, a name which is still given to a space between Waterloo Place and Leith Street. An ancient chapel, dedicated to St. Ninian, stood at its western extremity, and fragments of it existed in 1814, when the foundations of Waterloo Place were being prepared. The holy water font was removed by Mr. Walter Ross of Dean-haugh, and built into a tower which he erected on his grounds. On the demolition of the tower it was acquired by Sir Walter Scott, who transferred it to Abbotsford. This district formerly belonged to the family of Elphinston of Innerochtie, one of whom was created Lord Balmerino in 1603-4. In 1631 the then Lord Balmerino granted a charter to the trades of Calton, constituting them a society or corporation, and in 1669 a royal charter was obtained erecting the district into a burgh of barony.

Referring to the range of edifices swept away by the North British Railway, Dr. Daniel Wilson says:—" They were alto-
D

gether of a humble character, and appear to have very early
received a more appropriate dedication as 'The Beggar
Row.' One stone tenement, which seemed to lay claim to
somewhat higher pretensions than its frail lath and plaster
neighbours, owed its origin to the temporary prosperity of the
vassals of St. Crispin in this little barony. An ornamental
panel graced the front of its projecting staircase, decorated
with the shoemaker's arms, surrounded with a richly sculptured border, and bearing the pious motto, 'God Bliss Them
Cordiners, Wha Built this House.'"

St. Ninian's Row of old formed part of the road between the
city and the barony of Broughton, the road to Leith being
then by the way of the Canongate, Abbey Hill, and Easter
Road. Dr. Chambers in his "Traditions" says :—"The
origin of Leith Walk was accidental. At the approach of
Cromwell to Edinburgh, immediately after the battle of
Dunbar, Leslie, the Covenanting general, arranged the Scottish troops in a line, the right wing of which rested upon the
Calton Hill, and the left upon Leith, being designed for the
defence of these towns. A battery was erected at each extremity, and the line was itself defended by a trench and a
mound, the latter composed of the earth dug from the former.
Leslie himself took up his quarters at Broughton, whence some
of his despatches are dated. When the war shifted to another quarter this mound became a footway between the two
towns." In 1748 it was described as a gravel walk, 20 feet
in width, and no horses were allowed upon it. After the
erection of the North Bridge in 1749 it became a road,
and carriages passing over it, it soon became unserviceable.
About the beginning of this century it was covered with
road metal, and a toll erected where dues were exacted to
cover the expense incurred.

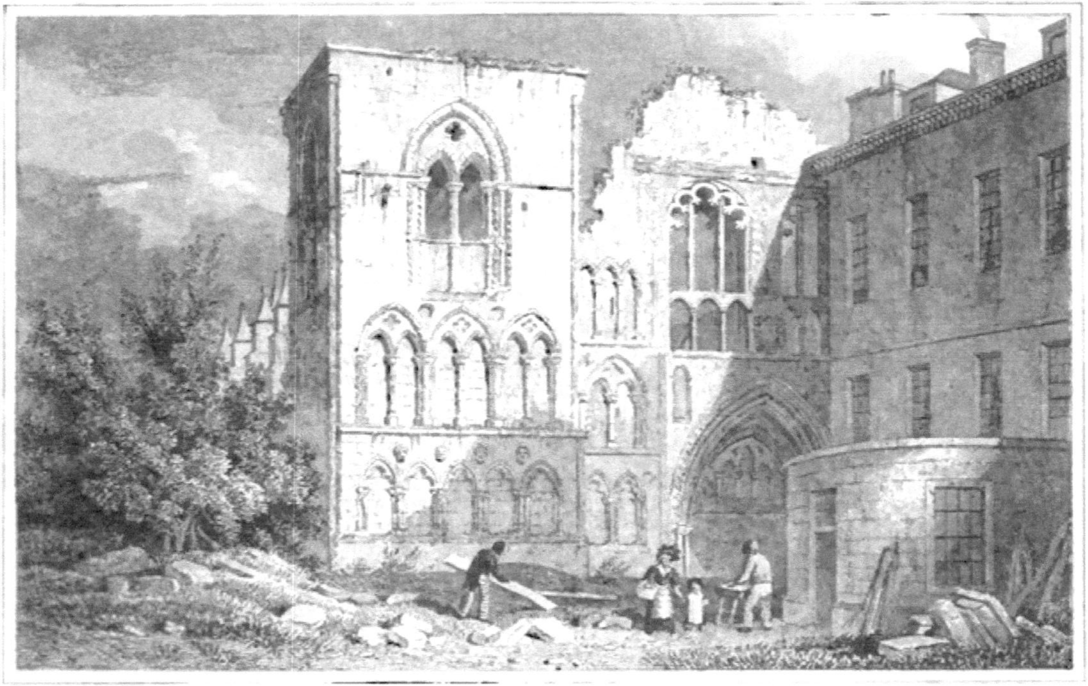

Drawn by Thos. H. Shepherd. Engraved by W. Tombleson.

HOLYROOD &c.

Holyrood Chapel.

THIS Chapel was founded by King David I. in 1128, and it is traditionally said to have been erected out of gratitude for the providential rescue of the King, while hunting in the forest of Drumsheuch, near the ravine of the Water of Leith. An infuriated stag charged him, but the miraculous appearance of a luminous cross in the sky scared the deer and saved the King. David endowed the Abbey, and subsequent monarchs and pious individuals further added to its revenue. The Abbot and Canons were invested with an extensive jurisdiction. The Abbey and the Collegiate buildings connected with it covered a large extent of ground, in fact "occupying more space than the Palace does now, and extending considerably further to the eastward; the more civil part of the building, as we learn from ancient description—the part devoted to the domestic uses of the Canons—consisting of several courts situated to the south of the Abbey church, and on the space occupied by the present Palace." The church originally appears to have been of noble proportions, while the decorations were rich and effective. What now remains is the nave of the ancient edifice, the choir and transept having disappeared. The finest portion of the Abbey is the west front, which bears traces of being the work of different ages. Dr. Wilson says " it has been curtailed of the south tower to admit of the completion of the quadrangle according to the design of Sir William Bruce, and the singular and unique windows over the great doorway are evidently additions of the time of Charles I., whose initials appear below, on the oak beam of the great doorway. The chief portions of the west front, however, are in the most beautiful style of Early English, which succeeded that of the Norman. The details on the west front of the tower, in particular, with its elaborately sculptured arcade, and boldly cut heads between the arches, and the singularly rich variety of ornament in the great doorway, altogether unite to form a specimen of early ecclesiastical architecture unsurpassed by any building of similar dimensions in the kingdom." The nave consists of eight bays with a side aisle. One circular arch remains on the south side of the aisle, undoubtedly a fragment of the original edifice. The eastern window is evidently of a much later date. The Chapel frequently suffered at the hands of the English. It was partially destroyed by Edward II. in 1332, burnt by Richard II. in 1385, and restored by Abbot Crawford in the time of James III., again to be demolished by the English under the command of the Earl of Hertford in 1544. Three years later Somerset the Protector ordered the monastery to be suppressed. Towards the close of the sixteenth century some of the buildings connected with the Chapel were removed to admit of the extension of the Palace. What remained of the Chapel was partially destroyed by a ruthless mob in 1688. It was, however, restored in 1758, but the stone roof gave way in 1768, filling the interior with rubbish. This was removed, and the building has since remained a magnificent ruin. Here many of the Scottish sovereigns were married, and the vault of the Chapel contains the remains of several of the Scottish kings. In 1848 the remains of Mary of Gueldres were deposited in the royal vault, after the demolition of Trinity College Church.

St. Anthony's Chapel.

THIS picturesque ruin stands on an elevated site, about a quarter of a mile from the Palace of Holyrood and on the north side of Arthur's Seat, commanding a view over Leith, the Firth of Forth, and the county of Fife. The Chapel was originally a Gothic building, 43 feet long, 18 broad, and 18 in height. At the west end was a tower, 19 feet square, and, it is supposed, before its fall, about 40 feet high. It is not known when the Chapel was erected, but it is generally believed to have formed a dependency of the Preceptory of St. Anthony at Leith. In the opinion of Dr. Daniel Wilson it was erected " to catch the seaman's eye as he entered the Firth, or departed on some long and perilous voyage, when his vows and offerings would be most freely made to the patron saint, and the hermit who ministered at his altar." Close to the Chapel are the ruins of the hermitage, partly formed out of the solid rock. Arnot, in his " History of Edinburgh," describing the hermitage as it appeared in 1779, says: " The cell of the hermitage yet remains. It is 16 feet long, 12 broad, and 8 high. The rock rises within two feet of the stone arch which forms its roof, and at the foot of the rock flows a fine stream." Little now remains of the cell but a small recess, with a stone ledge partly constructed out of the natural rock. According to an entry in the Lord Treasurer's accounts, James IV., on the 1st April 1505, gave 14s. " to St. Antoni's Chapell of the Crag."

A little below the Chapel is St. Anthony's Well, a spring of pure, cold water, which flows from underneath a huge boulder into a hollow stone basin, and which, in bygone

days, would doubtless be the source of supply for the uses of
the Chapel, and the occupant of the cell or hermitage. This
well has long been a favourite haunt of the citizens of Edinburgh on Sundays and holidays. The well is frequently
referred to in Scottish song, and in the pathetic ballad of
" Lord Jamie Douglas" occurs the following stanza :—

> " Now Arthur's Seat shall be my bed,
>   The sheets shall ne'er be pressed by me ;
> St. Anton's Well shall be my drink,
>   Since my true love's forsaken me !
> Martinmas wind, when wilt thou blaw,
>   An' shake the green leaves aff the tree ?
> O gentle death, when wilt thou come ?
>   For o' my life I am wearie."

Prince Charles, when he came to Holyrood in 1745,
traversed the Hunter's Bog, and "on reaching the eminence
below St. Anthony's Chapel and Well, when for the first
time he came in sight of the old palace, he alighted from
his horse, and paused to survey the beautiful scene. Then
descending to the Duke's Walk (so called because it had
been a favourite resort of his grandfather, to whose flagrant
misgovernment he owed his exile) he halted for a few
minutes to show himself to the people, who now flocked to
him in great numbers with mingled feelings of curiosity and
admiration. Loud huzzas came from the crowd, and many
of the enthusiastic Jacobites knelt down and kissed his hand.
He then mounted his horse—a fine bay gelding, presented
to him by the Duke of Perth—and rode slowly towards the
Palace. On arriving in front of Holyrood he alighted, and
was about to enter the royal dwelling, when a cannon ball
fired from the Castle struck the front of James V.'s tower, and
brought down a quantity of rubbish into the court-yard. No
injury was done, however, by this gratuitous act of annoyance."

547

Holyrood Palace.

THE attraction of the Abbey caused the Scottish kings frequently to visit this locality, and in course of time a portion of the Collegiate Buildings was set apart for the use of the Court. Here the Court frequently was accommodated before the erection of a palace by James IV. The King was betrothed to the Princess Margaret of England, and he was anxious to give her a grand reception upon her arrival in Scotland in 1503. Subsequently to these preparations the following entry occurs in the Records of the Privy Seal under date 10th September 1504:—"To Maister Leonard Logy, for his gude and thankful service done and to be done, to the Kingis hienis, and speciallie for his diligent and grete laboure made be him in the building of the palace beside the Abbey of the Holy Croce, the somme of forty pounds." This entry is the first authentic reference to the venerable Palace of Holyrood. The treasurer's accounts supply some interesting details regarding the progress of the Palace during the reigns of James IV. and V. On the 21st of January 1507 James V. was born in the Palace of Holyrood, and in 1537, Princess Magdalene, the daughter of Francis I. of France, was welcomed at Holyrood as his queen. She died, however, in the same year, and in 1538 James married Mary of Guise, the widow of the Duke of Longueville, and on her arrival at Holyrood after her marriage at St. Andrews she was received with great state. Queen Mary and her tragic history are closely connected with Holyrood. Her first trouble was her marriage to her unprincipled cousin, Darnley, which was quickly followed by the assassination of David Rizzio, her private secretary, whose reputed influence over the Queen aroused the enmity of a powerful section of the Scottish nobles. In the north-west portion of the Palace is shown the small room where the Italian was killed, and in an adjoining apartment some dark-coloured stains are said to mark the spot where his body lay before it was removed for burial. Dr. Wilson says: "The earliest drawing of the Abbey and Palace that exists is the bird's-eye view of 1544, where it is marked by its English draughtsman as 'the King of Skotts palis,' although the sole claimant to the throne at that date was the infant daughter of James V." The last evening Queen Mary was in Holyrood was that on which she was hurriedly taken away from the palace of her ancestors, and consigned to Lochleven Castle as a prisoner. Holyrood Palace was a favourite residence of James VI., and here his son Charles was baptized on the 23d December 1600, in presence of the nobles, heralds, and officers of state. On the occasion of James VI. revisiting Scotland in 1617, the Palace was decorated with considerable splendour. Taylor, the Water-Poet, in his "Pennylesse Pilgrimage to Scotland," in 1618, gives the following account of his visit to Holy-rood: "I was at his Majestie's Palace, a stately and princely seate, wherein I saw a sumptuous Chappell, most richly adorned with all appurtenances belonging to so sacred a place, or so royall an owner. In the inner court I saw the King's Armes cunningly carved in stone, over which was written this inscription in Latin: *Nobis hac invicta misecunt* 106 *Proavi*. I inquired what the English of it was. It was told me as followeth, which I thought worthy to be recorded: 106 *forefathers have left this to us uncon-quered.*" Taylor was in Edinburgh immediately after the visit of James VI. to Scotland.

The Palace was evidently abandoned to neglect and

decay after the last visit of Charles I., otherwise it is probable that Cromwell would have taken up his quarters there during his residence in Edinburgh. He, however, quartered some of his infantry in the Palace, when, owing to some carelessness, the greater part of it was destroyed by fire on the 13th November 1650. The north-west portion, or the Tower of James V., was saved, along with its fittings. Cromwell appears to have made some repairs on the Palace, but his work was pulled down at the Restoration, on the ground that it was "built by the usurper, and doth darken the Court." During the reign of Charles II. the reconstruction of the Palace was commenced by Sir William Bruce of Balcaskie, who was created a baronet in 1668, and it was probably about this time that he was instructed to prepare plans for the restoration of Holyrood. The first extant document relating to his designs is dated Windsor, June 3, 1671, when the Commissioners of the Exchequer were enjoined to allow Sir William to proceed with the work of restoration. These designs, according to the Earl of Lauderdale, had the approval of the King, who took special interest in the proposed appropriation of the Abbey Church, which the King intended should in future be the Chapel Royal, in place of the Chapel Royal in the Palace. This ecclesiastical building was of a semi-private nature, and it appears to have taken the place of the Chapel Royal at Stirling, where the kings of Scotland had been in the habit of attending public worship. The Chapel Royal appears to have been transferred to Holyrood about the year 1571. It was located in a building which had been used by the Court as a place of worship both before and after the Reformation. Mass had been celebrated in this chapel subsequent to Queen Mary's return in 1561; and Dr. Charles Rogers, in his exhaustive and painstaking work

on "The History of the Chapel Royal of Scotland," says:
" It was this fabric which became the Chapel Royal of
Scotland, in substitution for the deserted structure at
Stirling. The building was removed in 1671, when the
Palace was made to assume its present quadrangular form."

The Palace is a handsome and stately quadrangular
building, enclosing a square of 94 feet each way, surrounded by a piazza. The western front consists of two
double towers, connected by a two-storey architectural
screen, surmounted by a double balustrade and an octagonal
turret, with an open cupola in the form of an imperial
crown. The centre is pierced by the entrance gateway,
which is decorated with double columns of the Doric order.
The flat roof of this portion of the Palace distinguishes it
from the other sides of the building, which are three storeys
in height. The picture gallery, in which the election of representative peers takes place, is about 150 feet in length
by 27 in breadth. It is decorated with about 100 imaginary paintings of Scottish kings, executed by De Witt.
In the gallery are four paintings of considerable importance
and value: James III. and his son; his wife, Margaret of
Denmark; the Holy Trinity; and Sir Edward Bonkil, Provost of Trinity College Church, where the last two, along
with a third now lost, formed the altar-piece. These paintings were removed to England by James VII., and they
were returned from Hampton Court by order of the Queen
in 1862. In the northern and eastern portions of the
Palace are the royal apartments, which have occasionally
been used by the Queen during her visits to Scotland. In
front of the Palace is an ornate fountain with three ranges
of statuettes.

HIGH SCHOOL WYND

The South Bridge.

This Bridge is composed of twenty-two arches, of various sizes, the whole of which are concealed, except the one over the Cowgate. It runs in a line with the North Bridge, both of which intersect the High Street. From the regularity of the buildings, the largeness of the shops, and the great thoroughfare, this street may be considered the most compact, busy, and elegant of the Old Town. The foundation-stone of this bridge was laid in August 1785, and the whole was completed and the street opened in March 1788. In digging the foundation of the central pier of the Bridge, which was no less than twenty-two feet deep, many coins of Edward I., II., and III. were found. The old buildings which were removed to make way for this public work, were purchased at a trifling cost, while the areas on which they stood were sold by the city, to erect new buildings on each side of the Bridge, for £30,000. The Cowgate passes beneath the arch, and nearly the whole of this historical street can be seen from the bridge. This street was once a simple rural road, affording communication between Holyrood and the ancient church of St. Cuthbert at the north-west corner of the Castle rock. During the reign of James III. the Cowgate began to be a fashionable place of residence, and many pretentious mansions were erected in it. Here many of the nobility resided, whilst Cardinal Beaton had a palace at the bottom of Blackfriars Wynd, which in after years was the residence of Bishop Abernethy Drummond of the Scottish Episcopal Church, the husband of the heiress of Hawthornden. This palace has now been swept away to widen Blackfriars Wynd,

and such of the old houses that remain are now divided and
occupied by the very poorest of the working classes, most of
whom are natives of the sister island of Ireland.

At the foot of Niddry Street, close to the arch over the
Cowgate, is the building formerly known as St. Cecilia's
Hall, when concerts were given in its spacious hall. It
subsequently was the place where the meetings of the Grand
Lodge of Scotland were held, but for a considerable time it
has supplied accommodation for one of Dr. Bell's schools.
Mr. George Thomson, the friend and correspondent of Burns,
describing this hall, which was built in 1762 from a design
of Mr. Robert Mylne, after the model of the great open
theatre of Parma, says : " It was an exact oval, having a con-
cave elliptical ceiling, and was remarkable for the clear and
perfect conveyance of sounds, without responding echoes, as
well as for the judicious manner in which the seating was
arranged. A supper to the directors and their friends
generally followed the oratorio, where the names of the chief
beauties who had graced the hall were honoured by their
healths being drunk ; the champion of the lady whom he
proposed as his toast being sometimes challenged to maintain
the pre-eminence of her personal charms by the admirer of
another lady filling a glass of double depth to her health, and
thus forcing the champion of the first lady to *say more* by
drinking a still deeper bumper in honour of her beauty ; and
if this produced a rejoinder from the other by his seizing
and quaffing the cup of *largest* calibre, there the contest
generally ended, and the deepest drinker *saved* his lady, as
it was phrased, although he might have had some difficulty
in saving himself from a flooring while endeavouring to
regain his seat."

High School Wynd.

UNTIL the last few years, this was a narrow lane leading from the archiepiscopal palace in the Cowgate to Infirmary Street. The whole of the houses on the eastern side of the wynd have been taken down under the Improvement Act, and what was for long one of the most "picturesque bits" of Old Edinburgh is now nothing but a wide and precipitous thoroughfare. The fronts of these houses were mostly of wood, and they afforded one of the best specimens of the style of building which prevailed in Edinburgh in the sixteenth century. One of them, situated at the south-east corner of the Wynd, was a characteristic example. The house itself was built of stone, and the wooden projection extended to as far as the staircase, and was supported by wooden pillars. This building was also very peculiar in several other respects. Mr. Hunter, in his "Historical Sketches of Lady Yester's Church and Parish," says the house originally consisted of only one apartment, the partitions being of wood—leading to the belief that this was the first house built in 1554-55 for the accommodation of the High School, and that from it, and not from the two later buildings, the Wynd and adjacent High School Yards acquired the name by which they are still known. In the High School Yards the clergy of the Roman Catholic Church resided when their chapel was in a neighbouring wynd. The house of the Bishop was in the centre, and not many years ago "an elegant mantelpiece representing the Crucifixion was removed from the room which had been used by him as his study."

The High School Wynd was originally a narrow and rather lonely road leading to the Dominican Monastery, which stood on the site of the surgical wards of the Old Infirmary, and westward to the house of Kirk of Field, where Darnley was blown up. It was by this road that Bothwell and his fellow-conspirators went to perform the tragic deed which covers his name with well-merited ignominy, and has cast a dark cloud of suspicion upon the unfortunate Queen Mary, owing to her alleged complicity in the murder of her husband.

At the top of the Wynd, on the ground floor of a wooden-faced tenement, was the "Jib House," where the High Schools procured a home-made sweet, called *jube* or *jib*. Mr. Hunter says: "The *jib* not only enjoyed a great popularity among the boys, but many a penny was spent on it which was not intended to go there; many a copper was intrusted by the fairer portions of the family to their brothers to bring them a taste of the dainty sweetmeat; and, alas! many of the lads were under the necessity of rebutting the charge, sometimes with *striking* arguments, of having levied *black-mail* in its transit. It differed very materially from the common *quadie* or toffie, as it always retained a softness to which the other never could attain. Its original inventor was a Frenchman. It consisted of two parts of treacle and one of sugar, which were boiled together. In the length of time that the mixture was boiled, and the after manipulation, lay the secret of its retaining its softness. It was not flavoured at all; the boys having different tastes, some preferring one spice, and others a very different one. This will recall to memory the little basket of essences and pot of ground ginger which lay upon the table at the back of the shop, the rubbing of the cork of the selected bottle upon the jib, or the mixing of a quantity of the ginger with it."

Greyfriars' Church.

The Church of the Greyfriars was built by the magistrates of Edinburgh in 1612, on a portion of ground which formerly was part of the garden of the Monastery of the Franciscans or Grey-friars, which stood towards the Grassmarket, opposite the foot of the West Bow. This monastery, which was established by James I. in 1430, was demolished in 1559. Mr. Thomas G. Stevenson, in his work on "Old Edinburgh," says: "By the Reformation in Scotland, the monks and nuns were dispossessed of their lands. The Town Council, in the year 1561, made application to Queen Mary to grant to them the ground for the purpose of a public burying-place. In August 1562 she granted them this request, appointing the Greyfriars' Yard to be devoted to the use of the town for the specified purpose." The Church was built upon the upper part of the ground, and it had originally a spire or steeple which the magistrates used as a magazine for gunpowder. The spire was entirely destroyed by an explosion in 1718, but the magistrates, instead of rebuilding it, erected a new Church to the west, which was commenced in 1719, and finished in 1721. The old Greyfriars' Church was totally destroyed by fire on Sunday morning, 19th January 1845, and remained a roofless ruin until the year 1857, when it was repaired and opened for worship.

In the burying-ground are interred a large number of eminent men, including Principal Robertson, the historian; Allan Ramsay, Dr. Hugh Blair, Alexander Henderson, Dr. Pitcairn, Henry Mackenzie, author of "The Man of Feeling;" George Buchanan, the historian; Dr. Thomas M'Crie,

the biographer of John Knox; Dr. John Black, the chemist;
Professor Munro, Patrick Fraser Tytler, the historian; and
Lord President Forbes.

Dean Stanley, in his lectures on the Church of Scotland,
referring to this churchyard, says: "In this venerable
cemetery, which contains the dust of all the contending
factions of Scottish history—where the monument of the
Covenanters recounts their praises almost within sight of
the Grassmarket where they died; where rest the noblest
leaders, both of the moderate and of the stricter party, side
by side, another stately monument, at once the glory and
the shame of Scottish Liberals. It is the ponderous centre
tomb, bolted and barred, of Sir George Mackenzie, King's
Advocate under James II., and as such prosecutor of the
Covenanters."

The portion of the burying-ground extending south-
wards to Lauriston was used as an open-air prison for five
months in 1679, when several hundred of the Covenanters,
taken prisoners at Bothwell Bridge, were detained here
under circumstances of great privation. In the north-east
portion of the churchyard is the monument erected to the
memory of the martyrs during the religious persecutions in
Scotland. Beneath a lengthy poem on the stone is the
legend:

[From May 27th, 1661, that the Most Noble Marquis of
Argyle was beheaded, to the 17th of February 1688, that
Mr. James Renwick suffered, were one way or other Mur-
dered and Destroyed for the same Cause, about Eighteen
thousand, of whom were execute at Edinburgh about an
hundred of Noblemen, Gentlemen, Ministers, and Others,
noble Martyrs for JESUS CHRIST. The most of them
lie here.]

Trinity College Church.

THIS Church was founded in 1462 by Mary of Guelders, the widowed queen of James II., for a provost, eight prebends, and two singing boys, in addition to which the foundation had attached to it an hospital for thirteen bedemen, who were bound to pray for the soul of the foundress. The Queen-Dowager died the following year, and was buried within the edifice she had founded. The Church, which stood at the foot of Leith Wynd, was removed in 1848, to make way for the North British Railway. It was a fine specimen of the decorated English style of architecture. Describing the Church in 1847 before its removal, Dr. Daniel Wilson says, "The death of the Queen so soon after the date of the charter of foundation, probably prevented the completion of the Church according to the original design. As it now stands it consists of the choir and transepts, with the central tower partially built, and evidently hastily completed with crow-stepped gables and a slanting roof. The east end of the choir has a very stately and imposing effect. It is an apsis, with a lofty window in each of its three sides, originally filled with fine tracery, and not improbably with painted glass, though the only evidence of either that now remains is the broken ends of mullions and transoms. The ornamental details with which the Church abounds exhibit great variety of design, though many of those on the exterior are greatly injured by time. Various armorial bearings adorn different parts of the building, and particularly the east end of the choir. One of the latter has angels for supporters, but otherwise they are mostly too much decayed to be decipher-

E

able. One heraldic device, which from its sheltered position on the side of a buttress at the west angle of the south transept has escaped the general decay, is described by Maitland and Arnot as the arms of the foundress. It proves, however, to be the arms of her brother-in-law, Alexander Duke of Albany, who at the time of her decease was residing at the court of the Duke of Guelders. From the royal supporters still traceable, attached to a coat of arms sculptured on the north-east buttress of the vestry, the arms of the foundress would appear to have been placed on that part of the Church where she lies buried. In the foundation-charter it is specially appointed that, 'whenever any of the prebendaries shall read Mass, he shall, after the same, in his sacerdotal habiliments, repair to the tomb of the foundress with a sprinkler, and there devoutly read over the *De Profundis*, together with the *Fidelium*, and an exhortation to excite the people to devotion.' Many of the details of the Church are singularly grotesque. The monkey is repeated in all variety of positions in the gargoyles."

Shortly after the now veteran historian wrote the above accurate description of its characteristic features the Church was taken down, in spite of the protests of the Scottish Society of Antiquaries and other bodies. The stones of the Church lay for years on the slope of the Calton Hill, and it was fondly hoped that the edifice would be re-erected in another locality. After much litigation, it was finally decided by the House of Lords, that the only obligation resting upon the Town Council of Edinburgh was to erect a church for the parish with a portion of the money got from the Railway Company. A modern edifice was erected in Jeffrey Street in 1871-72. Attached thereto is the old apse, which has been restored *in toto*, whilst the ancient baptismal font of the old Church is placed in the lobby of the new edifice.

The Chapel of Ease, St. Cuthbert's.

THIS Chapel, now known as Buccleuch Street Church, is situated at the west end of the Crosscauseway. It was built in 1755 by public subscription, to provide accommodation for the population in the district, and was opened in the beginning of 1756. About ten years ago the Church was improved by the erection of a new front, at a cost of about £2000, when the Marquis of Bute erected a beautiful window to the memory of his ancestress, Flora Macleod of Raasay, who is interred in the burying-ground attached to the Chapel. In this quiet cemetery many distinguished citizens of Edinburgh have been buried, including Dr. Adam, the celebrated rector of the High School; David Herd, the ballad collector; Dr. Thomas Blacklock, the blind poet; and Mrs. Cockburn, the authoress of the modern version of "The Flowers of the Forest." It was in the open space in front of this Chapel that many of the street fights or "bickers" of stones between boys of different schools and localities took place, and which have been so graphically described by Sir Walter Scott in the general introduction to the Waverley Novels. Who has not read with fond enthusiasm Sir Walter's narrative of the famous battles between the George Square and Crosscauseway cohorts? Scott says, "It followed from our frequent opposition to each other, that, though not knowing the names of our enemies, we were yet well acquainted with their appearance, and had nicknames for the most remarkable of them. One very active and spirited boy might be considered as the principal leader in the cohort of the suburbs. He was, I suppose, thirteen or

fourteen years old, tall, blue-eyed, with long fair hair,
the very picture of a youthful Goth. This lad was always
first in the charge, and last in the retreat—the Achilles at
once and Ajax of the Crosscauseway. He was too for-
midable to us not to have a cognomen, and, like that of a
knight of old, it was taken from the most remarkable part
of his dress, being a pair of old green livery breeches,
which was the principal part of his clothing; for, like
Pentapolin, according to Don Quixote's account, Green
Breeks, as we called him, always entered the battle with
bare arms, legs and feet. It fell that, once upon a time,
when the combat was at the thickest, this plebeian champion
headed a sudden charge, so rapid and furious, that all fled
before him. He was several paces before his comrades, and
had actually laid his hands on the patrician standard, when
one of our party, whom some misjudging friend had intrusted with a *couteau de chasse*, or hanger, inspired with a
zeal for the honour of the corps worthy of Major Sturgeon
himself, struck poor Green Breeks over the head with
strength sufficient to cut him down. When this was seen,
the casualty was so far beyond what had ever taken place
before, that both parties fled different ways, leaving poor
Green Breeks, with his bright hair plentifully dabbled
in blood, to the care of the watchman, who (honest man)
took care not to know who had done the mischief. The
bloody hanger was flung into one of the Meadow ditches,
and solemn secrecy was sworn on all hands; but the
remorse and terror of the actor were beyond all bounds, and
his apprehensions of the most dreadful character. The
wounded hero was for a few days in the Infirmary, the
case being only a trifling one. But though inquiry was
strongly pressed on him, no argument could make him
indicate the person from whom he had received the wound."

68

Engraved by J. Barber

Surgeon Square.

THIS Square may now be said to have ceased to exist as one of the streets of the city, although two or three of the buildings which formed it still remain. The Square as it appeared about sixty years ago had an air of seclusion, as it was a *cul-de-sac*. It occupied the ground at the extremity of the High School Yards to the east of the Old High School, more recently the surgical ward of the Royal Infirmary, before its removal to the Meadows. The Square contained not only the Surgeon's Hall, but a commodious building for the use of the Royal Medical Society, and several handsome residences, latterly converted into medical and surgical lecture-rooms. The surgeons and barbers of Edinburgh were incorporated into a body by the Town Council on the 1st of July 1505, which was ratified the following year by a royal charter. In 1657, by their mutual desire, the surgeons and apothecaries were incorporated into one body. From this time pharmacy and surgery were united, and the barbers were not acknowledged as members of the corporation. " This occasioned an Act of Council of the 26th July 1682, recommending to this corporation to supply the town with a sufficient number of persons qualified to shave and cut hair, and who should continue dependent upon the surgeons. But in the year 1722 the surgeons and barbers were separated in all respects, except that the barbers were still obliged to enter their apprentices in the register kept by the surgeons." By a charter of George III. dated March 14th, 1778, this corporation was re-erected under the name of "The Royal College of Surgeons of the City of

Edinburgh." This charter established a scheme for the widows and children of members. By this scheme each member is obliged to pay £5 per year to the College during his life; if he dies before making four yearly payments, neither his wife nor children receive any benefit from the fund, but if he survives that period and leaves a widow, she is entitled to £25 per year during her widowhood: if he dies a widower leaving children, they are entitled in the whole to £100. The old hall of the surgeons was quite close to the city wall overlooking the north end of the Pleasance, and here all the meetings of the College were held until the erection of their new premises in Nicolson Street. The buildings belonging to the Medical Society are seen on the right side of Shepherd's view—they consisted of three large rooms, exclusive of smaller apartments. This Society has a large and valuable collection of medical books, which are now accommodated in their new rooms in Melbourne Place. Mr. George Sinclair of Ulbster, the father of the distinguished agriculturist, and the first baronet of the family, had a house in this Square. In this locality was the lecture room of the brilliant Dr. Robert Knox, who secured an unenviable notoriety in connection with the purchase of the bodies of the victims of Burke and Hare in 1828-29. Lord Cockburn, referring to these events in his " Memorials " of his time says: " All our anatomists incurred a most unjust and very alarming, although not an unnatural odium; Dr. Knox in particular, against whom not only the anger of the populace, but the condemnation of more intelligent persons was specially directed. But tried in reference to the invariable and necessary practice of the profession, our anatomists were spotlessly correct, and Knox the most correct of them all."

Lady Yester's Church.

THIS Church stands opposite the site of the Old Infirmary, in a street running eastward from the South Bridge. It owes its origin and name to the piety of Margaret Ker, Lady Yester, who in the year 1647 gave the citizens of Edinburgh 10,000 merks to build a church, and 5000 to be laid out towards the maintenance of a minister to officiate therein. The original Church, a representation of which is inserted in Gordon's Map of Edinburgh of date 1647, was a large and commodious edifice. The interior showed some features of interest, one of which was a wooden roof, with an elaborate representation of the final judgment upon it. During Cromwell's visit to Edinburgh, the Church somewhat suffered, as his soldiers pulled down many of the pews and made firewood of them. The original Church becoming insecure, it was taken down in 1803, and a new edifice erected in its place, a little to the west of the old site. The present Church has a fine window on the south front, but otherwise it presents no architectural details of interest. Principal William Robertson, the historian of Scotland, was for three years minister of this Church, and in more recent years among its ministers have been Principal Lee and Dr. John Caird, now the honoured Principal of the University of Glasgow. Dr. Hill Burton, sketching Principal Lee in "The Book Hunter," says: " We see him now—tall, straight, and meagre, but with a grim dignity in his air which warms into benignity as he inspects a pretty little clean Elzevir, or a tall portly Stephens, concluding his inward estimate of the prize with a peculiar grunting chuckle, known by the initiated to be an important announcement. Then, again, can we forget that occasion of his going to London to be examined by a committee of the House of Commons, when he suddenly disappeared with all his money in his pocket, and returned penniless, followed by a waggon containing 372 copies of rare editions of the Bible? All were fish that came to his net. At one time you might find him securing a minnow for sixpence at a stall, and presently afterwards he outbids some princely collector, and secures with frantic impetuosity, 'at any price,' a great fish he has been patiently watching for year after year. His hunting grounds were wide and distant, and there were mysterious rumours about the number of copies, all identically the same in edition and minor individualities, which he possessed of certain books. He was not remarkable for local attachment; and in moving from place to place, his spoil, packed in innumerable great boxes, sometimes followed him, to remain unreleased during the whole period of his tarrying in his new abode, so that they were removed to the next stage of his journey through life with modified inconvenience." James Paterson, who wrote the biographies accompanying Kay's Portraits, tells a good story of Mungo Watson, for many years beadle of this Church. He says: "Mr. Black, the minister of Lady Yester's Church, was perhaps the most popular preacher of his day; and strangers visiting the Church generally gave a trifle to the beadle to procure a seat. A gentleman had conformed to this practice in the forenoon, and returned to resume his seat in the afternoon, but was prevented by Mungo. The gentleman reminded him he had paid him in the forenoon. "Oh but," says Mungo, " I let my seats twice a day."

The University.

THE University of Edinburgh was founded by James VI. in 1582, and was originally located in an edifice which had belonged to the Collegiate Church of St. Mary-in-the-Fields. Before this, in 1558, Robert Reid bequeathed to the town of Edinburgh 8000 merks, for the purpose of erecting a University within the city; and Queen Mary, eight years later, caused a charter to be drawn, and a scheme devised for providing endowments for a College; but the unsettled state of the country prevented the inauguration of her well-meant plan. To the original College an addition was made in 1617, but the buildings had anything but an imposing appearance. The erection of the present structure was commenced in 1789, but it was not completed until 1834. The original design was supplied by Robert Adam, but it was extensively altered by Playfair, under whose superintendence the later portions were erected. The College forms a hollow parallelogram, 358 feet from east to west, and 255 feet from north to south, and having in the centre a large quadrangular court. The style within and without is of the Graeco-Italian order. The front is pierced by three grand and massive entrance archways, adorned by six noble Doric columns, each 26 feet high, formed of single blocks of Craigleith stone. The gateways are surmounted by a broad entablature, with the following inscription, cut in Roman letters:—

"Academia Jacobi VI., Scotorum Regis anno post Christum natum M.DLXXXII. instituta; annoque M.DCC.LXXXIX., renovari coepta, regnante Georgio III., principe munificen-

tessimo; Urbis Edinensis Præfecto Thoma Elder; Academiæ
Primario Gulielmo Robertson. Architecto Roberto Adam."

The Library Hall, 198 feet in length and 50 feet in
width, is a beautiful room, and contains about 150,000
volumes, which have gradually accumulated since its foundation by the bequest of Clement Little of his library, consisting of about 300 volumes. Drummond of Hawthornden,
the poet and historian, also bequeathed his library to the
University, whereby the College became possessed of a good
collection of our early literature. In the Hall of the Senatus
is a valuable collection of portraits, including Rollock, the
first Principal; John Knox, George Buchanan, Napier of
Merchiston, Principal Carstairs, Principal Leighton, and
General Reid, founder of the Chair of Music.

The University has a chancellor, who is elected for life,
a vice-chancellor, a rector; also a member of Parliament,
elected in conjunction with the University of St. Andrews.
The principal, who is elected by the curators, holds office
for life. There are four faculties in the University, respectively Arts, Theology, Law, and Medicine, and a staff of
forty professors. The average number of students in late
years has been fully three thousand, but by far the largest
proportion attend the medical classes. The large increase
of students and the necessity for accommodation to meet the
requirements of practical teaching in several departments
led to the inauguration of a movement for the erection of
additional class-rooms at Teviot Row, and the first portion
has recently been completed, from designs by Dr. Rowand
Anderson. The University Hall, the Tower, and other
portions have yet to be added, and when finished it will be
a handsome edifice, massive in proportion, and adapted to
meet all the requirements of a first-class University.

The Trades Maiden Hospital.

THE Trade Corporations of Edinburgh, excited by the example of the Merchant Company, became desirous to establish, for the daughters of their decayed members, an institution similar to the one founded by that body, under the title of the Merchant Maiden Hospital, when a contribution was accordingly made among the different companies of artificers in Edinburgh, and an hospital was fitted up about the year 1704 for the education and support of the daughters of decayed trades-burgesses. This establishment was ratified in Parliament, by an Act similar to that incorporating the Governors of the Merchant Maiden Hospital; and Mrs. Mary Erskine, the beneficent foundress of the above-mentioned institution, extended her charity in so liberal a manner to that destined for the daughters of tradesmen, that its Governors voted her joint-foundress of this Hospital also, and gave other testimonies of gratitude for her bounty.

The building represented by Shepherd stood on the east side of Argyle Square, close to the Independent Chapel, and was a plain three-storey structure, without any architectural characteristics, no portion of the Hospital funds having been devoted to ornamentation. It was removed to make way for the Museum of Science and Art. The Hospital is now located at Rillbank, on the south side of the Meadows.

Opposite to the Hospital was Minto House, latterly an hospital, but at one time the town residence of the Elliots of Minto. Under the management of Professor James Syme, Minto House became famous as a surgical hospital

for accidents and other cases. Subsequently it was used
by extra-mural lecturers, and was the scene of many important demonstrations. In Chambers Street a new building has been erected, which is also used by the extra-mural
medical lecturers, and the old and honoured traditions of the
school are retained in the same locality. On the site of the
Trades Maiden Hospital, the Independent Chapel, and the
south side of Argyle Square, is the Museum of Science and
Art, an extensive and imposing building now approaching
completion after many vexatious delays. The designs for
this structure was supplied by Captain Fowkes of the Royal
Engineers. The Museum contains extensive collections in
natural history, industrial art, in manufacture, and in matters
pertaining to the different branches of physical science. In
this locality also are the Heriot-Watt College, the Free
Tron Church, and the Training College of the Church of
Scotland. Argyle Square was built about 1730, and it is
said to have received its name from the following circumstance:—" A tailor, named Campbell, having got into the
graces of his chief, the great John, Duke of Argyle and
Greenwich, was promised the first favour that peer's acquaintance or interest might throw in his way. Accordingly, on the death of George I., the Duke having early
intelligence of the event, let his clansman, the tailor,
instantly know it, and the latter, before his brethren in the
trade were aware, bought up all the black cloth in the city,
and forthwith drove such a trade in supplying the zealous
Whigs with mourning suits at his own prices, that he
shortly realised a little fortune, wherewith he laid the
foundation of a greater. He began to build the first houses
of this Square, and named it Argyle in honour of his patron,
and much of it appears to have been finished when Edgar
drew his first plan of the city in 1742."

Methodist Chapel.

This commodious Chapel presents a handsome front to Nicolson Square, and it has an interior measure of 80 feet in length by 60 in width. It was erected by the Methodists in 1814, in place of a chapel removed to make way for the Regent Bridge. The cost, including the Minister's House and the Schools adjacent, was £5000. In close proximity to the Chapel there stood, until recent years, the house in which Thomas Campbell, the poet, resided for some time after he wrote "The Pleasures of Hope." Dr. Robert Chambers states that Campbell composed the poem in this house, but a study of Dr. Beattie's life of the poet shows that the famous poem was written in a humble dwelling in St. John's Hill, at that time a retired suburb. In this neighbourhood also, for several years, in a small house in General's Entry, resided Mrs. M'Lehose, better known as Clarinda, with whom Burns carried on a so-called Platonic correspondence. Clarinda, who had been deserted by a worthless husband, was a beautiful, vivacious woman, a clever conversationalist, and remarkably fond of company. Up to her death in 1841, she retained a profound admiration for Burns both as a man and a poet. She first met Burns towards the end of the year 1787, in the house of a mutual friend in the vicinity of her own dwelling. At this time Burns possibly considered himself free of all legal and moral obligation to Jean Armour, by the burning of her marriage lines, and her acquiescence in their destruction, as releasing him from the responsibility of wedlock. In these circumstances, says the grandson of Clarinda, Burns made her acquaintance, "and is it to be

wondered at that he found great delight in the society of a
lady of her talents and great vivacity,—well-read and fond
of poetry, romantic, and a 'bit of an enthusiast,' warm in her
feelings and attachments,—who immediately and keenly sym-
pathised with him? or is it a matter of surprise that he felt,
and sometimes expressed, hopes that were wild and visionary?"
As evidence of Clarinda's attachment to her friend, the following extract from her private journal may be quoted:—

"*6th Dec.* 1831.—This day I never can forget. Parted
with Burns in the year 1791, never more to meet in this
world.—Oh, may we meet in heaven!"

Behind this chapel is the Potterrow, a narrow street,
formerly one of the principal entrances to the city from the
south. It has still some buildings of historic interest, although many have been swept away. Towards the south end
there stood until recent years a range of buildings in the
decorated style of the reign of James VI., termed General's
Entry, which were supposed to have been built by Sir James
Dalrymple, the first Viscount Stair. Over one of the dormer
windows were the initials I. D., surrounded by beautiful
scroll work. Tradition says that General Monk resided in
this house while commander of the forces in Scotland, but
Dr. Wilson says: "It is not unlikely that the present name
of the old court is derived from the more recent residence
there of John, second Earl of Stair, who served during the
protracted campaigns of the Duke of Marlborough, and was
promoted to the rank of lieutenant-general after the bloody
victory of Malplaquet. He shared in the fall of the great
Duke, and retired from Court until the accession of George
I., during which interval it is probable that the family
mansion in the Potterrow formed the frequent abode of the
disgraced favourite."

Part of the New Town, from Ramsay Gardens.

THE point from which this view is taken is well calculated to show the characteristic features of the New Town.
Standing in the garden attached to the house of Allan
Ramsay the poet, the spectator commands a most extended
and diversified view of the New Town, as well as the outline
of the Fife coast. Near the centre is the Royal Institution,
situated at the north end of the Mound, whilst to the right is
a circular wooden building, which was used for the exhibition
of panoramas, but now removed. Speaking of the general
appearance of the Mound sixty years ago, Mr. Thomas G.
Stevenson, in "Edinburgh in the Olden Time," says: "Although
the earthen Mound was long previous to 1825 passable both
for foot-passengers and vehicles, the western portion of it
was allowed to remain comparatively waste and unprofitable,
occasionally made use of for exhibitions of wild animals and
other kinds of shows, circuses and panoramas; woodyards,
with a row of small wooden erections, occupied by carpenters,
masons, and bookbinders, together with a depot for road
metal and old building materials." The Mound is generally
supposed to have originated with George Boyd, a Lawnmarket hoiser, who, having frequently to go to the New
Town on business or pleasure, for his own convenience laid
down some pieces of wood, which enabled him to cross the
North Loch. Through time builders of houses in the New
Town got permission to deposit rubbish in the North Loch,
and foot-passengers gradually increased in number. In
1781–82 the magistrates of Edinburgh, in answer to a petition

calling attention to the inconvenience resulting from the
want of direct communication between the Lawnmarket and
Princes Street, "resolved to give every encouragement for
promoting a passage across the North Loch, from the Lawnmarket to Princes Street, and they accordingly ordered that,
until the said passage is completed, no materials of building,
stones, or earth, or rubbish, shall be laid on any streets,
closes, or avenues within or leading to the city, or upon any
part of the city's property except on that part of the extended
Royalty in the line of Hanover Street, next to the North
Loch, and upon the bank of the south side of the said North
Loch, immediately below the west end of James's Court, between the stakes now put up on both sides of the said loch."
With this encouragement, it is not surprising that the
quantity of earth excavated for the foundations of houses
and deposited here soon became enormous, and it is calculated
that a million and a half of cartloads were laid down between
1781 and 1830. The Mound is about 800 feet in length,
with an average breadth of 300 feet. Its height at the north
end is about 60 feet, increasing to 100 at the south. At the
head of the Mound is the Free Church College, built in
1846–50, after designs by W. H. Playfair, at a cost of
£40,000. The building is in the Tudor-Gothic style, and
has a fine quadrangle. There are nine class-rooms, a senate
hall, and a library hall. The library is rich in old theology,
including early editions of Calvin's works, John Knox's
Psalms, 1587; and Laud's Scottish Service Book. Amongst
the manuscripts are James Renwick's Dying Testimony, and
his Letter to his Christian Friends, 1688; several Wodrow
MSS.; the Autobiography of Thomas Boston; an unpublished
work of Vitringa on Church History; and the Lectures of
Principal Cunningham.

The Royal Institution.

THE Royal Institution, an elevation of which, before it was altered, is represented in the annexed engraving. It was erected for the accommodation of the Royal Society and the Society for the Encouragement of the Fine Arts in Scotland, the latter of which is now known as the Board of Manufactures. Owing to the nature of the ground on which it stands, it was considered necessary to lay the foundation upon piles, the cost for driving these amounting to about £1600. The building was commenced in 1825, after designs by W. H. Playfair, but it was not completed until 1836. It is oblong, of the Grecian Doric style of the time of Pericles. As represented by Shepherd, the building had no enrichment on the pediments, and a plain parapet surmounted the cornice. There were eight pedestals intended for statues between the flat Grecian pillars. Subsequently the building was altered and improved, and on the apex of the north pediment a colossal statue of the Queen, by Sir John Steell, was placed, accompanied by figures of sphinxes on the four angles. Dr. James Fergusson, speaking of this building in his "History of Architecture," says—"The porticoes cover the entrance, and the flank colonnades are stepped against blocks, which give them character and meaning, and the whole is well proportioned."

The Royal Society, which was incorporated by royal charter in 1783, grew out of several societies that had been established from time to time after 1731, when the "Society for Improving Medical Knowledge" was instituted. The first President of the Royal Society of Edinburgh was Henry

F

Duke of Buccleuch, and Professor John Robinson acted as secretary. The Society published the first volume of its Transactions in 1788, and this has been followed by numerous volumes, many of them containing papers describing important original researches in science.

The building also contains the National Museum of the Society of Antiquaries of Scotland, an important collection of prehistoric and historic relics. The specimens illustrative of the Stone, Bronze, and Iron periods or ages are varied and valuable, and they are so arranged as to supply students with materials for investigating the primitive civilisation of Scotland. Amongst the miscellaneous curiosities are *The Maiden*—the Scottish guillotine, the pistols used by Robert Burns as an exciseman, the folding-stool of Jenny Geddes, the ribbon worn by Prince Charles Edward as Knight of the Garter, the stool of penitence from Old Greyfriars' Church, and the sackcloth gown worn by penitents while standing on the stool, from West Calder Church.

To the south of the Royal Institution are the Art Galleries, built right over the railway tunnel which passes underneath the Mound. The foundation of this building was laid by the Prince Consort on the 31st of August 1850, and the galleries were opened in 1859. The design for the building was supplied by W. H. Playfair, and the cost was about £40,000. The structure, which is wrought out in the pure Doric style, is of an oblong form, with a beautiful Ionic portico. It contains two ranges of galleries. The western range is permanently devoted to the exhibition of a valuable collection of paintings illustrative both of the old masters and modern artists. One room is devoted to paintings by Scottish artists. The eastern range of galleries is used by the Royal Scottish Academy for its annual exhibitions of paintings.

Vegetable and Fish Market.

THE gallery of the Rainbow Coffee House afforded to Mr. Shepherd an opportunity of presenting a highly picturesque view of the above Market, which, up to a comparatively recent date, was held under the arches of the North Bridge. It was surrounded by covered stalls, principally occupied by vendors of salmon, trout, &c. The fishwomen from Newhaven and Fisherrow in their picturesque costumes assembled here, forming rows in the centre of the Market; and a scene of bustle and activity prevailed during the busy time, which was highly amusing to the passing stranger. The Vegetable and Fruit Markets occupied a part of the same area, and all the varieties of the season were exhibited in great abundance. The Vegetable Market was acquired by the North British Railway, and its site is now occupied by their platform and sheds. A new market, however, was substituted nearer Princes Street, on the site of the Edinburgh, Perth, and Dundee Railway Station. This Market, which is a large and commodious structure, has a flat roof, now utilised as a promenade and ornamental garden. The earlier market was situated on what was once a portion of the Nor' Loch. This loch extended from St. Cuthbert's Church on the west, to Halkerston's Wynd on the east. Dr. Robert Chambers, in the "Traditions of Edinburgh," says : "The lake, it after all appears, was artificial, being fed by springs under the Castle Rock, and retained by a dam at the foot of Halkerston's Wynd; which dam was a passable way from the city to the fields on the north. Bower, the continuator of Fordun, speaks of a tournament held on the

ground, *ubi nunc est lacus*, in 1396, by order of the Queen
(of Robert III.), at which her eldest son, Prince David, then
in his twentieth year, presided.   At the beginning of the
sixteenth century, a ford upon the North Loch is mentioned.
Archbishop Beatoun escaped across that ford in 1517,
when flying from the unlucky street skirmish called *Cleanse
the Causeway*.   In those early times, the Town Corporation
kept ducks and swans upon the loch for ornament's sake,
and various Acts occur in their register for preserving those
birds.   An Act, passed in Council between the years 1589
and 1594, ordained ' a boll of oats to be bought for feeding
the swans in the North Loch ; ' and a person was unlawed
at the same time for shooting a swan in the said loch, and
obliged to find another in its place.   The lake seems to
have been a favourite place for boating.   Various houses
in the neighbourhood had servitudes of the use of a boat
upon it ; and these, in later times, used to be employed to
no little purpose in smuggling whisky into the town."
With reference to the facilities afforded by the Nor' Loch
for smuggling, Sir Walter Scott in " The Heart of Mid-
Lothian" makes one of his characters say they enabled " an
honest man to fetch sae muckle as a bit anker o' brandy
frae Leith to the Lawnmarket, without being rubbit o' the
very gudes he'd bought and paid for by an host of idle
English gaugers."   Referring to the changes in connection
with the Nor' Loch, Chambers says : " Many in common
with myself must remember the by no means distant time
when the remains of this sheet of water, consisting of a few
pools, served as excellent sliding and skating ground in
winter, while their neglected grass-green precincts too frequently found an arena whereon the high and mighty
quarrels of Old and New Town *coolies* were brought to a
lapidarian arbitration."

The North Bridge, Calton Hill, &c., from the Bank of Scotland.

THIS Bridge and admirable design for connecting the two portions of Edinburgh naturally divided by the North Loch, is perhaps nowhere seen to greater advantage than from the station where the accompanying view was taken. The print also displays part of the Calton Hill and the buildings upon it in 1830. Among these are the Old and New Observatories, forming a group on the hill to the left; near the centre is the Cenotaph erected to the memory of Professor Playfair, to the right of which stands Nelson's Monument, having behind it the National Monument. On the lower part of the hill is another range or mass of modern buildings comprising the Jail, the Governor's House, and the Bridewell. The foreground to the left is formed by some of the houses of the New Town, whilst in the opposite side of the view are several of the buildings of the more ancient part of the city, connected by the Bridge, under and to the west of which was the market for fish and vegetables.

The foundation-stone of the North Bridge was laid on the 21st October 1763, by Lord Provost Drummond, who had recommended the adoption of a plan for forming a road from the Old Town to a district which was to be laid out for New Buildings. The North Loch was thoroughly drained and the mud removed; but nothing further was done until August 1765, when Mr. William Mylne, brother of the architect of Blackfriars' Bridge, London, gave designs, and contracted to complete the work before Martinmas 1769, for the sum of £10,140, and to uphold it for ten years. The undertaking was scarcely finished, when an accident occurred by which several lives were lost. The ridge against which the south end of the Bridge abutted is very steep, consisting in great part of earth which had been dug from the foundations of houses, and thrown down the declivity towards the loch. The architect had not made himself properly acquainted with the nature of the ground, and had neglected to go deep enough for a sound foundation. He had also failed to build the piers to a sufficient height, and was therefore obliged to place an immense mass of earth upon the arches (now bordered by tall tenements on both sides called North Bridge Street), in order to raise the Bridge to its requisite level. The result was that the side walls and abutments at the south end burst, and some of the vaults gave way, other parts having to be pulled down and rebuilt with chain bars. The superincumbent earth was removed, and its place supplied by small arches thrown between the convex sides of the great arches, and by throwing an arch of relief over the small south arch, which was shattered. Buttresses were also constructed at the north end, and these can still be seen in connection with the stair leading from the Bridge at the south end of the Post Office to the railway platform. In the course of time complaints were made regarding the narrowness of the Bridge, and as the outcome of numerous schemes, a plan was adopted whereby the carriage way and footpaths were considerably widened. This improvement was effected in 1873, under the superintendence of Messrs. Stevenson, the eminent engineers. The New Buildings, on the west side of the North Bridge, were erected between 1817 and 1819, and they occupy the site of Ann Street, a steep thoroughfare, which led from Princes Street to the now non-existent Canal Street. In this street the Ettrick Shepherd resided as the guest of John Grieve, a citizen of literary tastes.

86

Waterloo Place, The National and Nelson's Monuments.

THERE is no portion of the New Town of Edinburgh more worthy of graphic illustration than that represented in the annexed engraving. Public buildings, private houses, and national memorials, of varied design and styles of architecture, are here placed in juxtaposition, and altogether form a scene at once imposing and interesting. Nelson's Monument, a lofty tower, is one of the most prominent features, and in this view forms a pleasing termination to the vista, although the effect is somewhat marred by the proximity of the unfinished National Monument. From the eastern end of Waterloo Place, a flight of broad steps leads to the wide footpath which winds round the Calton Hill. In traversing this, the spectator views in succession the long lines of streets forming the New Town, bounded by Corstorphine Hill; the Firth of Forth, with the distant hills of Fife and Perthshire; the town and docks of Leith; the bay of Musselburgh, dominated by North Berwick Law; Arthur's Seat and Salisbury Crags, with Holyrood Palace and Abbey in the plain beneath; and lastly, the darkened and irregular masses of the Old Town, skirted and guarded on one side by the ancient Citadel.

The houses of Waterloo Place are divided by the Regent Bridge, which crosses the Low Calton and connects the hill with the ridge upon which the New Town is chiefly built. The Act of Parliament authorising the erection of this bridge, and the formation of the road from Princes Street to the east corner of the Calton Hill, certainly one of the most important of the recent improvements of Edinburgh, was passed in 1814. Prior to the erection of this bridge, the only communication from Princes Street to Portobello was by way of Leith Street, the Low Calton, and the North Back of the Canongate; Princes Street being then abruptly terminated by a row of houses running from Shakespeare Square to the top of Leith Street.

At the point of junction between Princes Street and Waterloo Place is the Register Office, which was built to preserve the records of Scotland. Previous to its erection, these national archives were in a state of disorder and decay; but they are now classified and arranged, and carefully guarded from further injury. A small portion of this building is seen to the left of the accompanying print. On the north side of the street is the Waterloo Hotel, one of the largest in Edinburgh. It contains, amongst other apartments, a dining room 80 feet by 40, a large coffee-room, and numerous other apartments. The expense of its erection was £30,000. More to the east, on the same side, is the Calton Convening Rooms, opposite to which are the Prison and the Old Calton Burying Ground. Near the latter is the General Post Office, now converted into a hotel, and further to the west the Stamp Office. The Theatre Royal, partially represented in the engraving, is marked by its portico, and by statues of Shakespeare and the Muses of Tragedy and Comedy, placed as acroters to the roof-pediment and its lateral copings. Although situated in a fine street, and close to several handsome public buildings, this theatre had a very mean appearance externally; the interior, however, was fitted up with some degree of attention to richness of effect.

The Register Office.

KING EDWARD I., thinking that he had reduced Scotland to subjection, and wishing, if possible, to destroy all remembrance of its name as a nation, abrogated its ancient laws, altered its religious worship, destroyed every historical record that fell into his hands, and carried away into England, not only all the books and writings he could find, but the learned men and teachers of learning, along with the stone chair of Scone, which might serve to remind the people of an ancient race of kings, intending not to leave a relic by which a patriotic feeling might be awakened. All the national records which had been collected from the time of Edward to the reign of Charles I. were seized by Cromwell and sent to the Tower of London. Part of these were returned at the Restoration, when one of the ships in which they were deposited was wrecked. These unfortunate occurrences have rendered the early part of the national history of Scotland comparatively obscure and imperfect.

In the year 1740 representations were made as to the necessity of acquiring apartments for the arrangement and preservation of the national records. The records were then said to be in "very bad condition, for want of boards to cover them; many of the first and last leafs of each book being so much obliterated as they cannot be easily read, and in a little time will be entirely defaced." James, Earl of Morton, while Lord Clerk Register, thinking it useless to hope for any direct government aid, obtained a grant of £12,000 out of the money received from the forfeited Jacobite estates, which, accumulating at interest till 1774, was appropriated to the building of this important public

edifice, the foundation-stone of which was laid that year.
The first portion of the undertaking was not completed
until 1783, and the remaining portions were finished
in 1822. This building, which cost about £80,000, was
designed by Robert Adam, and is considered one of the
finest works of that eminent architect. The front of 200
feet ranges from east to west, with a dome in the centre,
50 feet in diameter, and 80 feet high. The dome is
lighted by a window 15 feet in diameter, with a copper
frame-work. In the middle of the front four Corinthian
pilasters support a pediment, which bears the arms of
Great Britain on the tympanum. A turret at each end
projects a little beyond the rest of the building, with an
elegant Venetian window in front, and a cupola on the top,
surrounded by a stone balustrade. A Corinthian entablature,
of delicate workmanship, extends along the whole of the
front. The dome is used as a library, and there are about
100 vaulted rooms used for the conservation of the national
and legal records of Scotland. In one of the largest apartments are to be seen the rolls of ancient Parliaments, and
charters of the sovereigns of Scotland from William the
Lion to Queen Anne. Here also is preserved the Scottish
duplicate of the Treaty of Union. Amongst the offices are
those of the Register of Sasines, the Register of Deeds and
Protests, the Lord Privy Seal, and the Lyon King of Arms.

Partly behind the Old Register House is the New
Register House, built in 1857–60, after designs by Mr.
Robert Matheson, at a cost of £27,000. This edifice is
a good example of the Paladian style. The New House is
chiefly devoted to the preservation of the registers of births,
deaths, and marriages. In front of the Old Register House
is a fine bronze equestrian statue of the Duke of Wellington,
erected in 1852.

The Theatre Royal.

This building, which presented a very plain appearance when contrasted with the other public buildings of the city, was situated at the north end of the North Bridge, nearly opposite to the Register Office, on the site now occupied by the General Post Office. It was opened for performances in December 1769; the first manager being Mr. David Ross, formerly of the small theatre in the Canongate. The prices of admission at that time were 3s. for the boxes and pit, 2s. for the first gallery, and 1s. for the second or upper gallery. The house at these prices could hold with ease about £140, whilst its rival in the Canongate, when the prices were 2s. 6d., 1s. 6d., and 1s., was said to have held from £70 to £80. The Theatre was built in the field wherein Whitfield used to preach when he visited Edinburgh, and arriving while the building was in progress, he found that his favourite field was being appropriated to the service of Satan. The frantic astonishment of the Nixie, who finds her shrine and fountain desolated in her absence, was nothing to that of Whitfield. He went raging about the spot, and contemplated the rising walls of the playhouse with a sort of grim despair. He is said to have considered the circumstance as a positive mark of the increasing wickedness of society.

This Theatre was the scene of the great triumphs of Mrs. Siddons, and here also appeared Edmund Kean, Mrs. Yates, John Kemble, Charles Young, Charles Kemble, Macready, Mathews, Charles Kean, Helen Faucit, and other great actors and actresses. It was the leading Theatre in Edinburgh until 1859, when it was acquired by the Government, along with the surrounding houses of Shakespeare Square,

as a site for the Post Office. On the last night on which it
was open as a Theatre "Masks and Faces" was produced
with a very strong cast; the now popular Mr. Henry Irving
taking the subordinate part of "Soaper." Dr. Robert
Chambers, in a privately printed history of the Theatre-
Royal, referring to its palmy days, says: "It was indeed a
brilliant time for the house when it had Mr. H. Siddons for
Archer, Belcour, and Charles Surface; Mr. Terry for Sir
Peter Teazle, Sir Anthony Absolute, and Lord Ogleby; Mr.
Mason for stern guardians and snappish old men in general;
William Murray for almost anything requiring cleverness
and good sense; Mr. Berry for low comedy; Mrs. Henry
Siddons equally for Belvidera and Lady Teazle; Mrs. Nicol
for Mrs. Malaprop, and an endless variety of inexorable old
aunts and duennas; and Mrs. William Peirson for Audrey,
Priscilla Tomboy, and William in Rosina; when Joanna
Baillie had a play brought out on our stage, prologued by
Henry Mackenzie and epilogued by Scott; and whenever the
scenery and decorations were in the hands of artists of such
reputation as Mr. Nasmyth and Mr. J. F. Williams. Mrs.
Siddons came in March 1810. and performed a round of
her great parts—still appearing in the eyes of our fathers
the female Milton of the stage, as she had done twenty-six
years before in the eyes of their fathers. Mr. John Kemble
stalked on in July, the first time he had graced the boards
for ten years. But the glories of the season were not exhausted. The handsome Irish Johnstone, with his inimitable
Major O'Flaherty and Looney M'Twolter; Emery, with his
face like a great copper kettle, in such English rustic parts
as Tyke and John Lump; Mrs. Jordan, with her romping
vivacity and good-nature in the Country Girl and such
other parts, were among the rich treats presented to the
Edinburgh public in 1810."

The Post Office.

THE building represented in the annexed view was used as the General Post Office until 7th May 1866, when the present new and commodious office opposite the Register House was opened. The old office in Waterloo Place, now used as a hotel, was erected in 1821. In 1856 the staff of the Edinburgh office consisted of 225 officials, and Mr. Lang, in his "History of the Post Office in Scotland," says the average number of letters passing through and delivered daily in Edinburgh was estimated at 75,000, the number of mail bags despatched daily was 350, and the number received 518. Mr. Lang traces the gradual growth of the Post Office in Scotland from 1635—when the germ of the present system was established—down till a recent date. He states that "the first regular horse-post in Scotland appears to have been from Edinburgh to Stirling; it started for the first time on the 29th November 1715. It left Stirling at two o'clock afternoon, each Tuesday, Thursday, and Saturday, reaching Edinburgh in time for the night mail for England. In March 1717 the first horse-post between Edinburgh and Glasgow was established." This post left Edinburgh each Tuesday and Thursday at eight o'clock at night, and arrived in Glasgow the following morning at six o'clock in summer and eight o'clock in winter. A post was also despatched on the mornings of Sunday.

Dr. Robert Chambers, speaking of Post-Office arrangements in Edinburgh, says:—"Within the memory of an old citizen, who was living in 1823, the Post Office was in the first floor of a house near the Cross, above an alley which still bears

the name of the Post-Office Close. Thence it was removed
to a floor on the south side of the Parliament Square, which
was fitted up as a shop, and the letters were dealt across an
ordinary counter like other goods. At this time all the out-
of-door business of delivery was managed by one letter-
carrier. About 1745 the London bag brought on one occasion no more than a single letter, addressed to the British
Linen Company. From the Parliament Square the office was
removed to Lord Covington's house in the Parliament Close;
thence, after some years, to a house in North Bridge Street;
thence to Waterloo Place, and finally to a new and handsome structure on the North Bridge."

In connection with the Post Office, it may be stated that
in 1776 Peter Williamson established a penny post in Edinburgh, which became such a lucrative affair that the Post-
Office authorities paid him a handsome compensation to give
it up. Peter was kidnapped in early life, and sent to the
plantations, where he was captured by the North-American
Indians. He subsequently escaped, and returning to Scotland, commenced business as a vintner in a small shop at the
south-west corner of St. Giles's Church. In Peter's howff a
large amount of legal business was transacted in the closing
years of the last century. Williamson was also the first to
issue a Street Directory in Edinburgh.

The present Post Office occupies the site of the old Theatre-
Royal and Shakespeare Square, a locality full of memories of
quaint little taverns, oyster shops, and theatrical lodging-
houses. The edifice, which is Italian in style, was designed
by the late Robert Matheson of the Board of Works, and cost
about £120,000. The foundation-stone was laid by the late
Prince Consort on the 23d of October 1861, this being his
last appearance at any public ceremonial.

The Jail, from the Calton Hill.

THE Jail, as represented in the accompanying print, has a castellated character, although it is not in conformity to the military architecture of any distinct period. It consists of three different compartments. The central division includes the chapel, which is indicated in the print by three long windows. About 1830, when the sketch was taken, the ground floor was appropriated to the use of, and occupied by, six distinct classes; women-prisoners, debtors, untried men, and the remaining three by female convicts, having also an infirmary. A portion of the second storey of the building was occupied by the night cells, ranged on each side of long passages. The lower part of the central division was divided into separate cells for felons, and the gallery was appropriated to debtors. There were also four rooms used as infirmaries. The total number of cells in both stories was fifty-four. Each class of prisoners had a distinct open arcade for exercise, and also a court-yard. These connected at one point, where an octangular watch-house overlooked the whole. The building is surrounded by a massive wall, about twenty feet high, and the entry is by an embattled gate or lodge, surmounted by a platform, on which it was intended criminals should be executed.

An interesting object represented in the engraving is a castellated edifice called "The Jail Governor's House," overhanging one of the precipitous sides of the Calton Hill, and overlooking the various departments of the prison. This building was erected, together with the western division of the Jail, in 1815, from the designs and under the superintendence of Mr. Elliot, the architect, who carried into execution many of the modern improvements of Edinburgh. Romantically seated on the ledge of a rocky hill, its embattled turrets, parapets, and other architectural features, present an appearance at once imposing and picturesque. It has been objected by some persons, that this structure abounds too much in the caprices of the Gothic style of architecture. "But, surely," observes Sir Walter Scott in "The Provincial Antiquities of Scotland," "if the Gothic style can be anywhere adopted with propriety, the jail of a metropolis, built on the very verge of a precipice, and overhanging the buildings beneath like an ancient citadel, is the most appropriate subject for the purpose."

Among the groups of old houses on the east side of the Bridge there stood, until removed to provide station accommodation for the North British Railway, a plain-looking place of worship called Lady Glenorchy's Chapel and an edifice termed the College Kirk, but which was originally a collegiate church dedicated to the Holy Trinity, and founded, in 1452, by Mary of Gueldres, consort of King James the Second. More to the right was the Orphan Hospital, which Howard the philanthropist said was one of the most useful charities in Europe. This building was also swept away to make room for the railway, and the Hospital is now located in a handsome building near the Dean Cemetery. It is worthy of note that in the pediment between the two towers on the front of the Hospital is placed a peculiarly interesting relic of the past, in the shape of the ancient clock of the spire of the Nether Bow Port, which was demolished by the magistrates in 1764.

The New Bridewell, Salisbury Crags, and Arthur's Seat from the Calton Hill.

THE edifice which forms the principal feature in the annexed engraving, was constructed from the designs and under the superintendence of Mr. Robert Adam, architect. The foundation-stone was laid by the Earl of Morton, as Grand Master Mason of Scotland, on the 30th of November 1791, when the current coins, an almanac, newspapers, and a plate containing an inscription were deposited beneath it. This building was commenced when the public mind was much agitated, and the structure assuming a fortress-like appearance, the inhabitants of Edinburgh were suspicious that it would form a sort of bastile, and be used for secret and tyrannic purposes. It was completed for the reception of prisoners in 1796, at the expense of the city and county, aided by a grant of £5000 from the Government. The west part consists of a body with two projecting wings; and a central building also advanced before the main edifice. The upper part is embattled, and the angles are adorned with ornaments resembling small watch-turrets. The roof of the central portion of the Bridewell is flat, but the wings have embattled gables surmounted by crosses. The building, which is surrounded by a strong wall, has recently been enlarged and structurally altered.

Previous to the erection of the Bridewell, Edinburgh contained another edifice of the same nature, under the name of the House of Correction, in a building in Paul's Work, which had been erected in 1619 for the manufacture of woollen cloth, by tradesmen who had been brought

G

from Delft for the instruction of poor boys and girls in the art of weaving. The conduct of these strangers does not appear to have been altogether satisfactory, and Calderwood the historian records, in 1621: "Manie of the profainner sort of the toun were drawen out upon the sixt of May, to May games in Gilmertoun and Rosseline; so profanitie began to accompanie superstition and idolatrie, as it hath done in former times. Upon the first of May, the weavers in St. Paul's Worke, English and Dutche, set up a highe May pole, with their garlants and bells hanging at them, wherat was great concurse of people." This speculation was unsuccessful, and we next hear of the building when it was used as an hospital by General Leslie in 1650 for his sick and wounded soldiers, during the skirmishes that preceded his defeat at Dunbar. This building, which was removed to make way for the North British Railway, was "decorated with the city arms and sundry other rudely sculptured devices on the pediments of the dormer windows, and over the doorway was inscribed the pious aspiration: 'GOD · BLIS · THIS · WARK,' with the date 1619."

Another building in this neighbourhood is also designated Paul's Work. It was formerly the printing office of James Ballantyne & Co., the firm of which Sir Walter Scott was the principal partner. Here most of the Waverley Novels were printed, and in the house of Ballantyne, in St. John Street, were held many of those brilliant symposia at which the then "Great Unknown" read chapters of his forthcoming novels to select but sympathetic audiences. The collapse of the Constable and Ballantyne firms, in 1826, brought disaster to Sir Walter, and the closing years of his life were devoted to enforced literary work to raise funds to pay the liabilities for which he was responsible.

The High School.

THIS magnificent structure, from its situation, is one of the greatest ornaments to the City of Edinburgh. It is built on the Calton Hill, the solid rock being cut away to make room for its erection, on the north side of the Regent Road, which forms one of the finest approaches to the city. Our engraving is taken from the Canongate Churchyard, that being the only situation whence the eye can command the whole range of the building at one view, the road in front not showing such an extensive building to advantage. The Calton Hill rising behind, with Nelson's and the National Monuments on its summit, together with the old houses in the foreground, form a pleasing contrast with this elegant edifice. The foundation-stone was laid on the 28th of July 1825, by Viscount Glenorchy, Grand Master of the Freemasons in Scotland, attended by many noblemen, magistrates and officials, in the presence of an immense assemblage. The building is composed of a centre and two wings, together with two smaller buildings or lodges. The centre is a portico of six columns of the finest Grecian Doric, to which the wings are joined by a colonnade of the same order; it contains several large class-rooms, a common hall, library, and other apartments. The total cost of the building was upwards of £34,000, and the designs were supplied by Mr. Thomas Hamilton, architect. The erection of the building took five years, and when opened, in 1829, an imposing procession marched from the old school. Mr. John J. Hunter, in his "Historical Notices of Lady Yester's Church and Parish," describing the proceedings, says: "Great preparations were made for the occasion. It having been decided

that the pupils were to walk in procession from the old
school to the new, great pains were taken that they should
make a respectable appearance. For this purpose, a drill-
sergeant was engaged, and every day, for a considerable
time previous to that great event, the classes were suspended,
and the boys were initiated into the mysteries of marching
and counter-marching, forming four and two deep, taking
open order, lining the road, and again falling into their
places. The hatters invented a new bonnet to be worn on
the occasion; and many a parent was forced to consent to
his son being measured for the blue jacket and white ducks
which formed the almost uniform costume the boys assumed.
At length the eventful day arrived. The classes, for the
last time, assembled in their respective class-rooms, and were
afterwards marshalled four abreast, and side by side, in the
yards, by the late Sir Patrick Walker, Hereditary Usher of
the White Rod in Scotland. The preliminaries having been
adjusted, Sir Patrick waved his rod, and the pupils took
leave of the school in true schoolboy fashion, by giving
three hearty cheers in honour of their old *alma mater*. The
junior class walked first, preceded by the janitor in his
gown, and bearing his official baton. Two days after the
procession, the tablet, on which is inscribed the names of the
duxes of the school at the close of each session, was removed
to the new school — thus transferring all the honours of the
old school to it, and also closing its connection with Lady
Yester's parish." The previous High School, which was
erected in 1777, was, after the opening of the New School,
converted into the Surgical Hospital of the Royal Infirmary.
This building was erected close to the site of a previous
school, which was founded in 1578. From the entries in
the Town Council Records in connection with the original
school, it must have been a very shabby edifice.

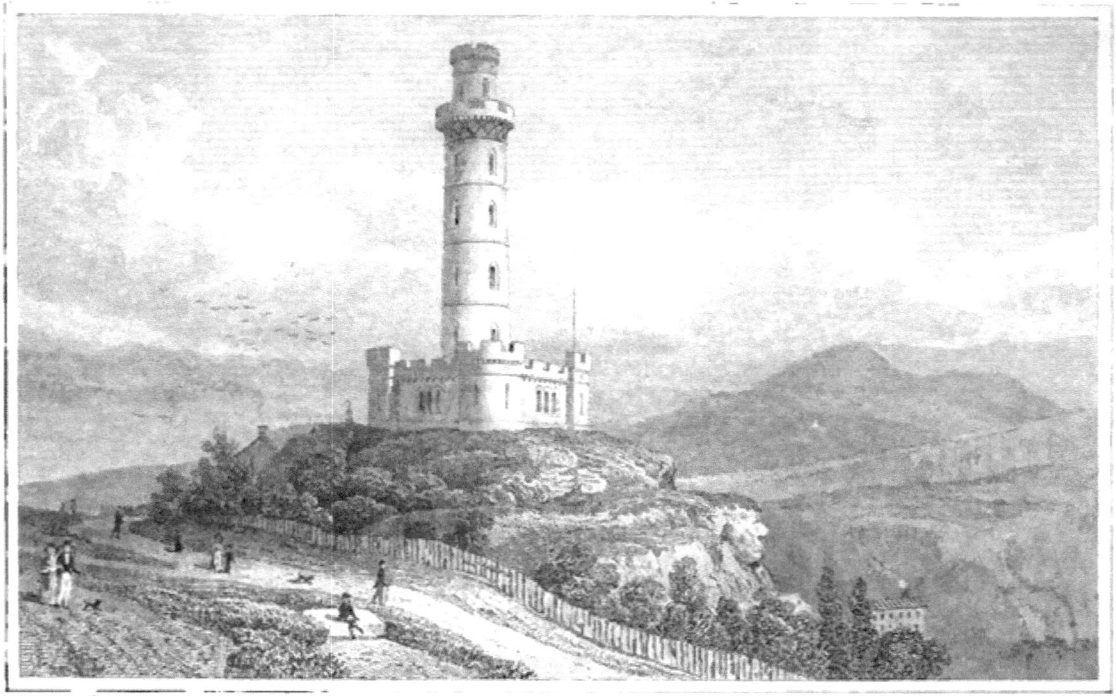

Drawn by [illegible] Engraved by W. Tombleson

Nelson's Monument.

On the highest point of the Calton Hill stands the monument erected to commemorate the gallant services to his country of Admiral Lord Viscount Nelson. The base is pentangular in form, surmounted by a circular tower 100 feet in height, which has been frequently compared to a butter churn. The top of the tower is battlemented, and on it is placed a time-ball and a flagstaff. Over the doorway are the Nelson crest, a piece of sculpture representing the stern of the *San Josef*, and an inscription recording that the citizens of Edinburgh "have erected this monument, not to express their unavailing sorrow for his death, nor yet to celebrate the matchless glories of his life, but by his noble example to teach their sons to emulate what they admire, and, like him, when duty requires it, to die for their country." The column is surrounded by a well-kept shrubbery, in which is planted three Russian cannons, trophies of the Crimean War.

From the top of the monument a magnificent view is obtained of the salient features of the rapidly-expanding cities of Edinburgh and Leith, now virtually one ; the hoary Castle, the picturesque Arthur's Seat and Salisbury Crags, the long range of the Pentlands, the richly-cultivated lands of the Lothians, as well as the wide sweep of the Firth of Forth, thickly studded with passing vessels, and the serrated outline of the Fife coast.

To the west is the Royal Observatory, a small building erected from a design by Mr. W. H. Playfair in 1818. The building presents the form of a cross of 62 feet,

with four projecting pediments of 28 feet each, supported
by six Doric columns, fronting the four points of the
compass. A dome 13 feet in diameter, forms the centre
of the building, under which is a conical pillar of solid
masonry, built of Craigleith sandstone, and resting on the
earth-fast porphyritic trap rock which forms the summit of
the hill. The chief instruments of the Observatory are an
8-foot transit instrument, and a 6-foot mural circle, both
mounted in the meridian. There are also a train of sidereal
clocks under electric control, and a train of electrically con-
trolled mean time clocks, of which the governing clock is
daily adjusted to the tenth of a second, in accordance with
the results of nightly star observations made with the transit
instrument, and this train of clocks extends from the Observatory over the whole city of Edinburgh, including in its
course clocks at the General Post Office, the University, and
the Museum of Science and Art, which are the centres again
of subsidiary clock-circles, besides the specially electric-con-
trolled clock which fires the time-gun daily at the Castle, whose
distance is about 4000 feet south-west from the Calton Hill.
The Astronomer-Royal is at present Professor Piazzi Smyth,
to one of whose volumes of astronomical observations we
are indebted for some of the foregoing details regarding
the Observatory.

Behind the Observatory is a rock vault, closed by a gate,
and termed the Jews' burial place. There is no record how
the vault came into the possession of the Jewish community,
and the authorities of the Edinburgh synagogue are only
aware of two individuals, a man and his wife, having been
buried in the cavern.

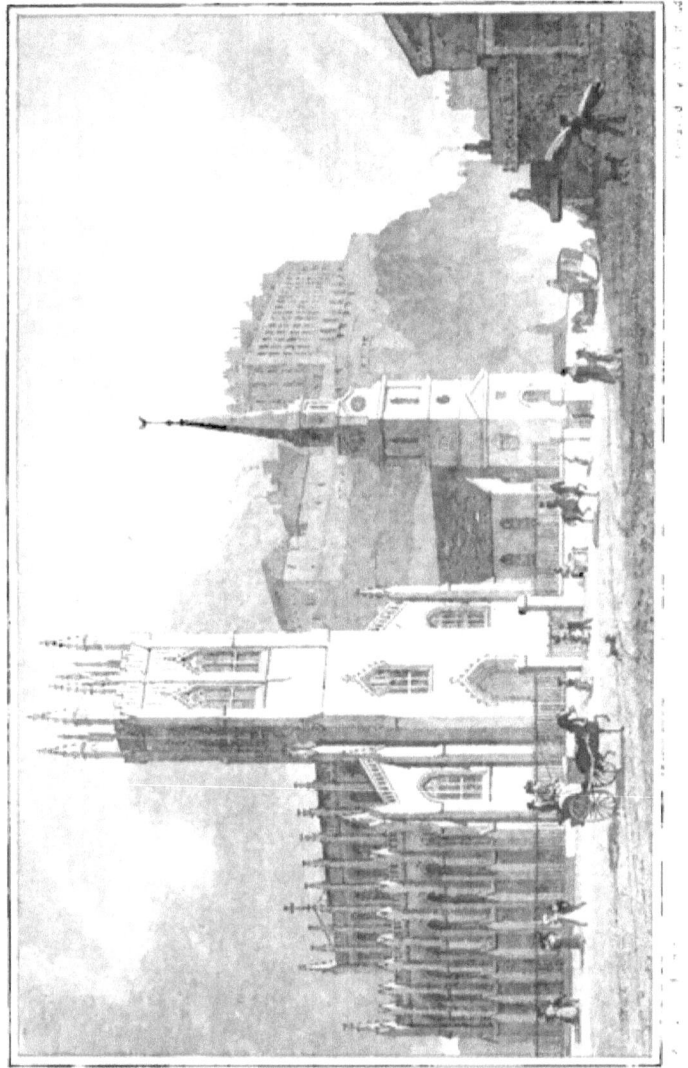

St. John's Chapel, St. Cuthbert's Church, &c.

St. John's is a beautiful Episcopal Chapel, situated at the western extremity of Princes Street. It was founded in 1816, and finished in 1818, at an expense of about £18,000. It was designed by Mr. William Burn, and is a good specimen of the florid description of Gothic architecture. It is 113 feet in length, by 62 in breadth. On the west it is terminated by a slightly projecting and elegant tower, 120 feet in height, surmounted by turrets. Through this tower is the principal entrance by a beautifully arched Gothic door. The north and south walls of the Chapel are richly buttressed, and are terminated by a cornice and battlement; each of the compartments between the buttresses, with the exception of the two eastmost, being occupied by a window. The inner walls, which are divided and ornamented in a similar manner with the outer ones, are terminated by rows of small Gothic turrets. The windows between the buttresses are of stained glass. The great eastern window, which is 30 feet in height, contains figures of the Twelve Apostles by Eggington, of Birmingham. Below the Chapel on the north side is a range of arched burial vaults, and there is a cemetery in the ground around the Chapel. The Chapel has no gallery, and the roof is supported by two rows of light and elegant Gothic columns. In the vaults and little cemetery are interred the remains of many persons of rank and eminence. Among them are Sir William Hamilton, Sir Henry Raeburn, James Donald-son, printer, the founder of the hospital which bears his name; Dr. Andrew Thomson, of St. George's Church; the

Rev. Archibald Alison, and Dr. Pulteney Alison, his son;
Mr. Macvey Napier, editor of the *Edinburgh Review;* Miss
Catherine Sinclair, and Professor Laycock.   Outside, at the
east end of the Chapel, is a fine cross erected to the memory
of Dean Ramsay, who for many years officiated in the
adjoining building.

A little to the south of St. John's Chapel, which occupies
the foreground of the plate, is St. Cuthbert's, or the West
Church : the parish church of the most populous parish in
Scotland.   It is a very plain building, and contrasts somewhat unfavourably with its splendid Episcopalian neighbour.
It was built in 1774-75, on the same spot which had been
occupied for centuries before by the former church of the
same name, which had successively been a Roman Catholic,
Presbyterian, Episcopalian, and finally a Presbyterian place
of worship.   The Church has two large galleries, and can
accommodate about 3000 persons.   In a secluded portion
of the churchyard is the tomb of Thomas de Quincey, one of
the greatest prose writers this country has produced.   The
Rev. David Williamson, an incumbent of this Church at the
Revolution of 1688, is generally credited with being the
" Dainty Davie " of Scottish song.   Williamson, it is stated,
had seven wives, and the last, Jean Straiton, survived him.

Referring to the barracks in his " Letter to the Lord
Provost on the Best Ways of Spoiling the Beauty of Edinburgh," Lord Cockburn says, " Look at the west side of the
Castle and shudder.   No doubt it was the Government that
reared this factory-looking erection which deforms the most
picturesque fortress in her Majesty's British dominions, by
the most audacious piece of abomination in Europe.   But
was Government instructed ?   I have been told that there
was not a public murmur at the time.   At any rate, there
it is—lofty and offensive."

St. George's Church and the West Side of Charlotte Square.

THE Square, a portion of which is represented in the
accompanying print, forms the western termination of
George Street, and was constructed from the designs of
Robert Adam, who is said to have exerted the fullest effort
of his powers to make it an elegant street. In this he has
in a great measure succeeded; and had his designs for the
Church, which is the chief ornament in this quadrangular
mass of buildings, been adopted, few squares in the kingdom
would have rivalled this in architectural composition and
effect. So strictly did the magistrates and trustees appointed
for carrying into effect the plans for the construction of the
New Town adhere to Mr. Adam's elevations in the erection
of houses, that one gentleman, who had constructed a
dwelling on the east side of the Square from the designs of
another architect, was compelled to pull it down, and re-
erect it according to the original design: although, in the
opinion of competent judges, the front was much better
than any of the adjacent buildings. Mr. Adam's design
was taken partly from the west front of St. Paul's Cathedral,
London, but was rejected on account of the expense attending its execution, and a building made up from the shreds
and patches, designed by Mr. Robert Reid, was commenced
in 1811 and completed in 1814, at an expense of £33,000.
The building, as seen from the Square, consists of a recessed
vestibule, supported by Ionic columns, elevated on steps,
and surmounted by a balustrade. The vestibule is flanked
by wings of a plain and massive style of architecture; and
from behind it, on a basement 48 feet square, rises a dome

with a lantern and cross, in imitation of that of St. Paul's Church, London. The total length of the façade towards the Square is 112 feet; the breadth of the steps, 68 feet; the height of the columns 35, and the summit of the cross from the ground, 160 feet. The vestibule is supported by four columns and two pilasters of the Ionic order. The dome by which the building is surmounted is considered too large for the façade. The first minister of this Church was Dr. Andrew Thomson, so well known by his labours in the cause of negro emancipation.

In one of the houses of this Square resided Sir William Fettes, Bart., of Comely Bank, at one time a grocer in the High Street, at the head of Bailie Fyfe's Close. He acquired a competency as a contractor for military stores, and purchased various estates from time to time. He bequeathed the residue of his estate to "form an endowment for the maintenance, education, and outfit of young people whose parents have either died without leaving sufficient funds for that purpose, or who from innocent misfortune during their own lives are unable to give suitable education to their children." The trust funds at Sir William's death in 1836 amounted to £166,000, and they remained at interest until 1864, when the trustees commenced the erection of the elegant and commodious College at Comely Bank. In the centre of the Square is the Albert Memorial, designed by Sir John Steell. This structure includes an equestrian statue of the Prince, surrounded by groups of figures representing the different classes of the community. The memorial was inaugurated by the Queen in August 1876, when there was an imposing ceremony.

The Assembly Rooms.

THE first Public Assemblies in Edinburgh were held in 1710, when a private association was instituted, which was located in a humble edifice in the West Bow, once the residence of a branch of the Sommerville family. In those days dancing was held in abhorrence by the great body of the Presbyterians, and it is not surprising to find that the votaries of the "poetry of motion" were persecuted by the populace. Jackson, in his "History of the Stage," says on one occasion the company in the West Bow rooms were assaulted by an infuriated rabble, and the door of their hall perforated with red-hot spits. About 1720, the Assemblies were removed to a building between Borthwick's Close and the Old Assembly Close, destroyed in the great fire of 1824. When studying medicine at the University of Edinburgh, Oliver Goldsmith was in the habit of frequenting these select Assemblies, and he gives a vivid sketch of the gatherings in a letter written to a friend in 1753. "Let me say something," writes Goldsmith, "of their balls, which are very frequent here. When a stranger enters the dancing-hall he sees one end of the room taken up with the ladies, who sit dismally in a group by themselves; on the other end stand their pensive partners that are to be: but no more intercourse between the two sexes than between two countries at war. The ladies, indeed, may ogle, and the gentlemen sigh, but an embargo is laid upon any closer commerce. At length, to interrupt hostilities, the lady-directress, intendant, or what you will, pitches on a gentleman and a lady to walk a minuet, which they perform with a formality approaching to despondence. After five or six couples have thus walked the gauntlet, all stand up to country dances, each gentleman furnished with a partner from the aforesaid lady-directress. So they dance much and say nothing, and thus concludes our Assembly."

In 1766 the Assemblies were transferred to an improved room then erected in Bell's Wynd. Here it was that the Hon. Miss Nicky Murray, one of the sisters of the Earl of Mansfield, acted as directress, and many stories are told of the kindly despotism displayed by her in managing the dancing in accordance with the etiquette of the period and the limited capacity of the room. The ladies were brought down the close in sedan chairs, and after being deposited in the lobby, they had the opportunity of purchasing gloves from a reduced gentleman who claimed to be Lord Kirkcudbright. This locality becoming both inconvenient and unfashionable for the Assemblies, a movement was inaugurated for the erection of a new and more commodious room in George Street. The cost was raised by subscription, and the room was finished in 1787. Externally the Assembly Room is a building of considerable elegance, the front of which is ornamented by an arcade and a pediment. The ballroom is 92 feet long, 42 feet wide, and 40 feet in height. Before the erection of the adjoining Music Hall in 1843, numerous banquets were held in the Assembly Room. In March 1816, the citizens of Edinburgh entertained the Black Watch to a banquet upon its return to Edinburgh Castle after Waterloo, and a few years afterwards the Ross-shire Buffs were similarly honoured. It was at the banquet of the Edinburgh Theatrical Fund Association, held in the Assembly Room, that Sir Walter Scott announced the already partially revealed secret that he was the author of " The Waverley Novels."

The Physicians' Hall.

THE Royal College of Physicians of Scotland was incorporated on St. Andrew's Day 1681 by a charter of Charles II., ratified by Parliament in 1685. At the time of its institution, Edinburgh, according to Maitland, had become the prey of "foreign impostors, quacks, empirics, and illiterate persons, both men and women, who, without the least knowledge of that learned science, audaciously presumed to practise as physicians, not only to the scandal of that noble art, but to the great danger and destruction of the health and lives of his Majesty's subjects." The extermination of these male and female characters was one great motive for the institution of the College. The Charter ordained that the College should consist of certain individuals who were named, and of all others who might be chosen by them as Colleagues and Fellows of their Society within the city of Edinburgh, its suburbs and liberties; so that they and their successors should be united and conjoined into one body, community, and college, in all time coming. The College was also empowered to authorise occasional examinations of the medicines kept in the apothecaries' shops, and to condemn and throw into the street such as were not found to be of good quality. To give leisure to attend on their patients, the Charter provided that no members of the College should be cited as a juror in any assize in town or country, and they were also relieved from being called out to watch or ward. It is uncertain where the first meetings of the College were held, the early minutes having been lost. In 1704 the College purchased the house and grounds of Sir James

Mackenzie in the Fountain Close. The College converted
some ruinous buildings towards the Cowgate into a pavilion-
shaped cold bath, " which was open to the inhabitants generally, at a charge for each ablution of twelve shillings Scots
and one penny to the servant. At first a committee of the
Physicians appears to have attended to receive the fees and
superintend the ablutions." In 1722 a new hall was erected
in the garden, but this in course of time proved insufficient.

The next Hall where the College met to deliberate matters
relating to the profession was erected in 1775-6 on a site at
the east end of George Street, immediately opposite St.
Andrew's Church, and was a handsome Grecian structure.
The principal entrance, which was reached by a flight of
steps, was decorated with a projecting portico, supported
by four Corinthian columns 24 feet in length. When a
small portion of the New Town was erected, it was proposed
by some of the Lady Directresses of the Edinburgh Assemblies, then held in dingy apartments in a close in the High
Street, to purchase the Hall and convert it into Assembly
Rooms. The project, however, fell to the ground, when the
Directresses came to consider the remoteness of the locality
from the residences of the greater part of them, and the
dangers they might incur by the overturn of their sedan
chairs, while going home, over the bridge just erected to span
the Nor' Loch, in the early hours of a wintry morning. In
1843 the Hall was sold to the Commercial Bank for £20,000,
a sum which enabled the College of Physicians to erect a
handsome Hall in Queen Street, containing apartments for
an extensive library, and a valuable museum of Materia
Medica. The Bank removed the Hall, and erected on its site
a magnificent edifice of mingled Greek and Roman character,
designed by the late Mr. David Rhind.

George Street, St. Andrew's Church, and Lord Melville's Monument.

GEORGE STREET divides the original New Town into two nearly equal parts, and is itself intersected at regular intervals by Hanover Street, Frederick Street, and Castle Street. It is terminated to the east by St. Andrew Square, and to the west by Charlotte Square. The public buildings which it contained in 1830 were St. Andrew's Church on the north side, the Physicians' Hall, nearly opposite, on the south, and the Assembly Rooms on the same side, more to the west. For regularity and uniformity of design this street was not then surpassed by any other in the Metropolis. It has recently been greatly improved by the erection of several handsome banks and insurance offices, and statues of George IV., Pitt, and Dr. Chalmers, at the points where it is crossed by Hanover, Frederick, and Castle Streets, and the noble and artistic Albert Memorial in the centre of Charlotte Square. The principal edifice represented in the accompanying print is St. Andrew's Church, marked by its fine tapering spire, and a bold portico supported by Corinthian columns. In the distance is seen part of St. Andrew Square, in the centre of which, forming a pleasing termination to the street, is the column raised to commemorate Lord Melville and his services to the country; whilst in the background stands the Royal Bank of Scotland.

St. Andrew's Church, which was the first place of worship erected in the New Town, was built in 1784, from a design supplied by Major Fraser of the Engineers. The church cost £7000, and has nearly 1100 sittings. The spire, which is 168 feet in height, was added three years later, from a design by William Sibbald, architect. It was in this church, in 1843. that the General Assembly was held, when the Disruption took place which led to the formation of the Free Church. When Lord Brougham visited Edinburgh in October 1859, on his appointment as Chancellor of the University of Edinburgh, he resolved to attend forenoon service in St. Andrew's Church on the Fast Day. Mr. G. Bruce, W.S., in his " Notes on the History of St. Andrew's Church," describing the incident, says: "On entering the lobby, which he did after most of the congregation had gone in, his nephew proposed to him to go up to the gallery to the pew then occupied by Lord Justice-Clerk Inglis. He declined, and told his nephew to go there, but he would go to a pew below in the centre of the church. He asked the elders attending the collection-plate if he could obtain a seat there. One of them happened beforehand to hear of his intention to visit the church, and having ascertained the pew in which he used to sit, arranged that there should be a vacant place left in it. He accordingly directed the beadle to show his Lordship to pew No. 28. Lord Brougham was shown into it, and afterwards mentioned this to a friend as a curious coincidence, and as having afforded pleasure to him. When the last psalm or paraphrase was given out, an old lady who was next him in the seat, and who did not know who he was, observing him turning over the leaves of the paraphrases, and thinking he was strange to the service, and could not find the place, offered assistance. He declined this, and after service was over told her he knew well how to find the psalm, but he was looking out the paraphrases (Nos. xxv., xlii., and xliii.) written by his great-grandfather, the Rev. Mr. Robertson, minister of Old Greyfriars."

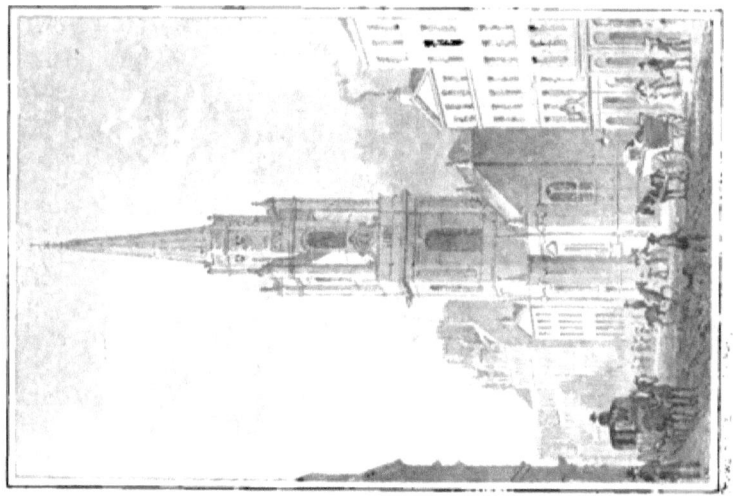

The Tron Church.

THE Tron Church, or Christ's Church at the Tron, occupies a very commanding situation in the High Street, where it is intersected by the North and South Bridges. It appears to have been founded in 1637, but owing to the expense incurred in the erection of this and another church then in process of construction on the Castle Hill, to supply the wants of the increasing population, the buildings proceeded slowly. Doubtless the political circumstances of the time had something to do with this delay, as the incomplete church on the Castle Hill was thrown down by Cromwell's soldiers, and the stones possibly were used for the construction of redoubts for his artillery during the siege of the Castle. In 1644 the Town Council ordered a large quantity of copper from Amsterdam to cover the roof, but altering their plan, the metal was sold, and instructions given to cover the roof with lead and slates. In 1647 the Church was so far completed as to admit of worship being conducted within its walls, but it was not entirely finished until 1663. The Church, which is a fair specimen of the Scottish renaissance style of architecture, cost £6000.

In 1673, a bell which cost 1490 merks Scots was hung in the steeple, and five years later the old clock which belonged to the Tron or Weigh House was placed in the tower. The spire, which was constructed of wood, was burned in 1824, during the great fire which nearly destroyed the whole range of buildings between Parliament Square and the Tron Church.

When the South Bridge was erected in 1785, the east end of the Church, and a large and stately range of build-

H

ings which abutted on it, were removed. Wilson says: " A
large archway in this building, immediately adjoining the
Church, formed the entrance to Marlin's Wynd, in front of
which a row of six stones, forming the shape of a coffin,
indicated the grave of Marlin, a Frenchman who, having
first paved the High Street in the sixteenth century, seems
to have considered that useful work his best public monument; but the changes effected on this locality have long
since obliterated the pavior's simple memorial." On the
vacant space to the west of the Tron Church, and forming
the entrance to Hunter Square, stood the Black Turnpike,
described by Maitland as one of the most magnificent buildings in Edinburgh. This house was the residence of Sir
Simon Preston of Craigmillar. He was provost of Edinburgh in 1567. and hither Queen Mary was brought a
prisoner after her surrender at Carberry Hill. In her passage through the city the Queen was insulted by the mob,
and, referring to this incident in his Life of Kirkaldy of
Grange, Mr. James Grant says: " Mary's face was pale
from fear and grief; her eyes were swollen with tears; her
auburn hair hung in disorder about her shoulders; her fair
form was poorly attired in a riding-tunic; she was exhausted
with fatigue, and covered with the summer dust of the
roadway, agitated by the march of so many men; in short,
she was scarcely recognisable; yet thus, like some vile
criminal led to execution, she was conducted to the house
of Sir Simon Preston of Craigmillar. The soldiers of the
confederates were long of passing through the gates; the
crowd was so dense, and the streets were so narrow, that
they filed through man by man." After passing a night
in this mansion, the Queen was taken to Holyrood, deprived
of her ornaments, and despatched the following evening to
Lochleven Castle, in charge of two of the confederate lords.

Lord Melville's Monument.

In the centre of St. Andrew Square stands a monument to the memory of the first Viscount Melville. This structure, which consists of pedestal, pillar and statue, rising to the height of about 150 feet, was erected in 1821, after a design by Mr. William Burn, at a cost of £8000. The pillar is modelled after the celebrated Trajan column at Rome, but is fluted and not ornamented with sculpture. The statue which surmounts the pillar is 14 feet high. The expense of the structure, as the inscription on the plate of pure gold deposited in the foundation-stone states, was met by the voluntary contributions of the officers, petty officers, seamen and marines of these united kingdoms. The foundation-stone was laid in 1821, on the anniversary of Lord Melville's birthday, by Admiral Sir David Milne.

Lord Melville was a member of the celebrated Dundas family. He was Lord Advocate in 1775, and filled some high posts in the Government of Great Britain during the reign of William Pitt. He was raised to the peerage in 1802, and shortly afterwards was charged with misappropriating the funds which passed through his hands in virtue of his office of Treasurer of the Navy. He was tried before his peers in Westminster Hall in 1806, when the evidence adduced not implicating him in the alleged malversations, his Lordship was, by large majorities, acquitted on all the charges. Lockhart, in his "Life of Sir Walter Scott," referring to the excitement which this trial caused in Scotland, says: "The impeachment of Lord Melville was among the first measures of the new (Whig) Government; and personal affection and gratitude graced as well as heightened the zeal with which Scott watched the issue of this—in his eyes—vindictive proceeding ; but though the ex-Minister's ultimate acquittal was, as to all the charges involving his personal honour, complete, it must be allowed that the investigation brought out many circumstances by no means creditable to his discretion—and the rejoicings ought not, therefore, to have been scornfully jubilant. Such they were, however—at least in Edinburgh ; and Scott took his full share in them by inditing a song, which was sung by James Ballantyne at a public dinner given in honour of the event, 27th June 1806." One verse may be quoted :—

> " Since here we are set in array round the table,
> Five hundred good fellows well met in a hall,
> Come listen, brave boys, and I'll sing as I'm able,
> How innocence triumphed and pride got a fall."

Mr. James Paterson, in his biography of Lord Melville in " Kay's Portraits," tells the following story regarding the discomfiture of his Lordship by the witty Harry Erskine:— 'During the Coalition Administration, the Hon. Henry Erskine held the office of Lord Advocate of Scotland. He succeeded Dundas (the future Viscount Melville), and on the morning of his appointment he met the latter in the Outer House, when, observing that Dundas had already resumed the ordinary stuff gown which advocates generally wear, he said, gaily, 'I must leave off talking, and go and order my silk gown,' the official costume of the Lord Advocate and the Solicitor-General. 'It is hardly worth while,' said Mr. Dundas, drily, 'for all the time you will want it : you had better borrow mine.' Erskine's retort was very smart. 'From the readiness with which you make the offer, Dundas, I have no doubt the gown is made to *fit any party ;* but it shall never be said of Harry Erskine that he put on the *abandoned habits* of his predecessor.' "

The Royal Bank.

THE building occupied by the Royal Bank was originally built at the expense, and for the residence, of Sir Laurence Dundas, for many years the representative of the City of Edinburgh in Parliament, and the founder of the branch of the Dundas family represented by the Earl of Zetland. The house was planned by Sir William Chambers, architect, on the model of a much-admired villa near Rome. The Bank is situated in a recess on the east side of St. Andrew Square, of which it forms one of the chief ornaments. It is a square building, three stories high. In the front is a rusticated basement, from which rise four pilasters with Corinthian capitals, supporting an entablature and pediment; and on the tympanum of the latter are cut the armorial bearings of the first proprietor of the building. It was sold to the Government at the end of the last century, and was occupied by the Board of Excise for a considerable time before it passed into the hands of the Bank, who paid the Government £33,000 for the house. When first established by charter in 1727, the stock of the Royal Bank amounted to about £110,000. That sum, however, having been found insufficient, another charter was procured in 1738, by which the directors were authorised to increase their stock to £150,000, and they were subsequently empowered to raise the amount to £1,000,000.

In the centre of the vacant space in front of the Bank is the Hopetoun monument, in memory of General Sir John Hope, afterwards fourth Earl of Hopetoun, who died in 1823. Sir John was colonel of the Gordon Highlanders,

and saw some stirring service in the Peninsular War. After
the fall of Sir John Moore, General Hope assumed the
command of the British army at Corunna. The design for
the monument, which comprises a bronze statue in Roman
costume leaning on a pawing charger, was supplied by
Campbell.

Somewhere between the site of the Register Office and
the Royal Bank stood a cottage with a signboard " Peace
and Plenty," where " curds and cream " and fruits in their
season were sold. This humble place of entertainment was
much frequented by the citizens of Edinburgh on summer
evenings. It was situated on a straggling road, which,
starting from the east of Princes Street, wound its way in a
slanting direction through the fields to Silvermills, and
thence to Stockbridge. A portion of it was called Gabriel's
Road, which subsequently became transformed into West
Register Street. It contained two noted taverns—Ambrose's
and Gabriel's. The former of these is the scene of the
famous imaginary wit-contests of "Christopher North"
and his associates, known as the *Noctes Ambrosianæ*, and
which were for a considerable time one of the characteristic
features of *Blackwood's Magazine*. In these racy dialogues,
Wilson puts into the mouth of Hogg sayings which are inimitable for humour, fanciful exaggeration, and pathos; but as
opinions were attributed to the Shepherd which he professed
to repudiate, there followed an interruption of the friendly
relations which had previously subsisted between Blackwood
and Hogg. Through the intervention of Wilson, Hogg
apologised to Blackwood for some unfounded statements he
had made, and the friendship was resumed on its old footing,
much to the credit of all parties.

East Side of St. Andrew Square.

In Shepherd's view of the east side of St. Andrew Square, there is little to note in the way of changes, except the removal of one of the mansions to make way for the British Linen Company's Bank, an ornate structure erected in 1851–52, from designs by David Bryce, R.S.A., at a cost of £30,000. The building is surmounted by six statues, each 8 feet in height, above a series of fluted projecting Corinthian columns. They represent Navigation, Commerce, Art, Science, and Agriculture. Adjoining is the National Bank, a plain fronted edifice, with a large telling-room to the back. To the north of the Royal Bank was the Douglas Hotel, now the head office of the Scottish Provident Institution. This hotel was one of the fashionable places of resort in Edinburgh, and was patronised by the nobility. The Empress Eugenie and the Prince and Princess of Wales at one time resided in it. The house was built by Andrew Crosbie, a noted Edinburgh lawyer, the prototype of Sir Walter Scott's Councillor Pleydell in "Guy Mannering." Crosbie was a man of undoubted ability, and acquired some wealth as the result of a successful practice. He was a regular frequenter of the famous drinking taverns of Clerihew and Douglas in the closes of the High Street. In his closing years he suffered great reverses, which forced him to retire to the High Street, where he died in penury.

Dr. Robert Chambers, in his "Illustrations of the Author of Waverley," tells the following story regarding Crosbie : "It is recorded of him that he was one day particularly brilliant—so brilliant as even to surprise his usual audience,

the imperturbable lords themselves. What rendered the
circumstance more wonderful was, that the case happened
to be extremely dull, commonplace, and uninteresting.
The secret history of the matter was to the following effect:
—A facetious contemporary and intimate friend of Mr.
Crosbie, the celebrated Lord Gardenstone, in the course of
a walk from Morningside, where he resided, fell into conversation with a farmer, who was going to Edinburgh in
order to hear his cause pleaded that forenoon by Mr. Crosbie.
The senator, who was a very homely and rather eccentric
personage, on being made acquainted with the man's business, directed him to procure a dozen or two farthings at a
snuff-shop in the Grassmarket, to wrap them separately up
in white paper, under the disguise of guineas, and to present them to his counsel as fees, when occasion served.
The case was called. Mr. Crosbie rose; but his heart not
happening to be particularly engaged, he did not by any
means exert the utmost of his powers. The treacherous
client, however, kept close behind his back, and ever and
anon, as he perceived Mr. Crosbie bringing his voice to a
cadence, for the purpose of closing the argument, slipped
the other farthing into his hand. The repeated application
of this silent encouragement so far stimulated the advocate,
that, in the end, he became truly eloquent, strained every
nerve of his soul in grateful zeal for the interests of so good
a client, and, precisely at the fourteenth farthing, gained
the cause. The *denouement* of the conspiracy took place
immediately after in John's Coffee House, over a bottle of
wine, with which Mr. Crosbie treated Lord Gardenstone
from the profits of his pleading, and the surprise and
mortification of the barrister, when, on putting his hand
into his pocket in order to pay the reckoning, he discovered
the real extent of his fee, can only be imagined."

Engraved by W. Watkins

St. George's Chapel, York Place.

THE building represented in the annexed engraving is situated on the south side of York Place. The street is wide and open, but the houses are neither remarkable for their size nor for their architectural embellishments; and the only public building it contains, besides the one here delineated, is St. Paul's Chapel, a modern Gothic edifice. St. George's Chapel was erected in 1794 from the designs of Mr. Robert Adam. The main building is a regular octagon, having in front a square porch, flanked by covered passages, which form a sort of screen to the Chapel. The architecture cannot be considered to belong to any regular order, as windows of the earliest pointed style are placed in juxtaposition with those of the eighteenth century; and ornaments of the time of Henry VIII. are contrasted with pinnacles and battlements which, however original, are not particularly harmonious. The interior of the building is neatly fitted up; the pulpit and reading desk occupy the two southern angles, with the altar behind them. The Chapel, which can accommodate 650 worshippers, cost £2200.

Nearly opposite this Chapel is the house and gallery erected by Sir Henry Raeburn, the distinguished portrait-painter, and as his influence on the development of art in Scotland has been so great, Allan Cunningham's description of his studio and method of working will be perused with interest :—

"Though his painting-rooms were in York Place, his dwelling-house was at St. Bernard's, near Stockbridge, overlooking the Water of Leith, a romantic place. The steep banks were then finely wooded, the garden grounds

varied and beautiful, and all the seclusion of the country
could be enjoyed without the remoteness. The motions
of the artist were as regular as those of a clock. He rose
at seven during summer, took breakfast about eight with
his wife and children, walked up to his great room in 32
York Place, and was ready for a sitter by nine; and of
sitters he generally had, for many years, not fewer than
three or four a day. To these he gave an hour and a
half each. He seldom kept a sitter more than two hours,
unless the person happened—and that was often the case—
to be gifted with more than common talents : he then felt
himself happy, and never failed to detain the party till
the arrival of a new sitter intimated that he must be
gone. For a head size he generally required four or five
sittings: and he preferred painting the head and hands
to any other part of the body, assigning as a reason that
they required least consideration. A fold of drapery, or
the natural ease which the casting of a mantle over the
shoulder demanded, occasioned him more perplexing study
than a head full of thought and imagination. Such was
the intuition with which he penetrated at once to the
mind, that the first sitting rarely came to a close without
his having seized strongly on the character and disposition
of the individual."

Among the other noted residents in York Place were
Lord Craig, the cousin-german of Mrs. M'Lehose, the
"Clarinda" of Burns ; Dr. John Abercrombie, Admiral Sir
David Milne, Lord Newton, a member of the famous Croch-
allan Club; Alexander Osborne, a man of immense stature ;
and Lady Sinclair of Murkle. One of the present residents
in the street is Mr. James T. Gibson-Craig, a noted book and
picture collector, whose rich stores fill all the rooms of his
large dwelling.

St. Paul's.

ST. PAUL'S is an Episcopal chapel, situated on the north side of York Place. It is of minute and florid Gothic architecture, of a kind similar to that exhibited in King's College Chapel, Cambridge. The chapel consists of a nave and two side aisles. The angles of the nave are marked externally by four handsome octagonal embattled towers. The south wall, which fronts York Place, is buttressed, and adorned with a row of Gothic turrets with crockets, connected with each other by a close embattlement. Above, and parallel to these, and marking the southern limit of the nave, is a range of similar turrets, united by open embattled work. The pulpit and altar are in the east end of the chapel, which faces Broughton Street. The interior dimensions of the chapel are 105 feet by 63 feet. One of the angles is occupied by the vestry. The nave is roofed by a flat Gothic arch, ornamented with rich tracery work. The aisle roofs are furnished and adorned in a similar style. The building is after a plan furnished by Mr. Archibald Elliot. It was finished in 1818, and cost £12,000, the sum being raised by voluntary subscription among the members of the congregation. At the time Shepherd took his sketch, the incumbents were the Rev. Archibald Alison, father of Sir Archibald Alison the historian, and the Rev. Robert Morehead.

At the west end of the Chapel is a lane leading northwards to the last existing portion of the old village of the Barony of Broughton. Mr. Mackay, in his "History of the Barony of Broughton," says: "The village, from the very meagre accounts which we have been enabled to obtain of it,

appears to have been situated principally to the north of
what is now Albany Street, and comprised within its limits
the sites of the streets known as Broughton Place and Street,
Barony Street, Old Broughton, and Albany Street. The
houses, with few exceptions, were two stories in height,
though small, having outside stairs, thatched roofs, latterly
tile, and crow-stepped gables, each cottage having a small
plot of ground or kail-yard in front. They seem to have
been placed along both sides of a road or pathway running
east and west—the greater number of the houses standing
on the north side. Those on the south side of the road
apparently had been more detached—spread between the
pathway and what now forms the site of Albany Street, and
up to York Place. There were also a number of houses at
the west end of the village, forming, as it were, the side of a
square. These were afterwards cut through when Broughton
Market was made. A few of the houses may still be seen
there, but they are now modernised, while some fragments
of the walls of others, to the east and west of these, remain
at the present time." At what is now the north-east corner
of Barony Street was the Broughton Tolbooth, a quaint two-
storey edifice, built in 1582. The structure was removed in
1829, but some of the lower walls of the building exist in
the shape of cellars in a public-house.

To the east of the Chapel, on the site of Picardy Place,
was the little hamlet of Picardy, which stood till the close
of the last century. It was built for a colony of French
weavers, who are said to have fled to this country after the
revocation of the Edict of Nantes in 1685. They planted
mulberry trees, and attempted to produce silk. The mulberry plantations were, however, a failure, and the emigrants
appear subsequently to have become linen-weavers.

Catholic Chapel.

THIS Chapel is situated at the south end of Broughton Street, immediately adjoining the Theatre Royal. It was built in 1813 from a design by Mr. Gillespie Graham, architect, at an expense of £8000. Much of the architectural ornamentation, however, exhibited on Mr. Gillespie's plan was not executed, on account of the insufficiency of the building fund. In consequence of the proximity of the chapel to the surrounding buildings, the eastern front is the only portion of it which comes prominently into view. This front, however, is surmounted by two central pinnacles 70 feet in height. This Chapel is now the Pro-Cathedral of the Archbishop of St. Andrews and Edinburgh, and since the appointment of Dr. William Smith it has been slightly enlarged, with a view to adapt it to the requirements of the Roman Catholic body, which of late years has largely increased in Edinburgh. The Chapel possesses a very fine organ, and above the altar is a large painting, by Vandyck, of a Dead Saviour, presented by Miss Chalmers, daughter of Sir George Chalmers. It is stated that George IV., when he saw this painting in London, in the course of its transit from the Continent to Edinburgh, was so much impressed by it that he offered £3000 for the work. Of course no transaction took place, as the Bishop declined to part with the gift. Amongst the effects belonging to the Chapel are a set of candlesticks used at Holyrood during the short reign of James II. of England, and some pieces of altar plate presented about 1831 by one of the French princes at that time resident at Holyrood, and who took his first communion at this Chapel. The interior dimensions of the Chapel are 110 feet by 57. Some dignitaries of the Roman Catholic Church lie buried before the high altar, including Bishops Cameron, Paterson, and Carruthers, and Archbishop Strain.

Adjoining the Chapel is the Theatre Royal, which occupies the site of the Theatre erected here in 1792 by Stephen Kemble, who had been unsuccessful in his attempt to obtain the management of the Theatre in Shakespeare Square. The new house, which was termed a circus, was opened in January 1793, when Sheridan's comedy of *The Rivals* was produced. The then lessee of the other Theatre obtained an interdict against Kemble for performing stage plays without a license. Kemble, however, the same year secured a lease of the Shakespeare Square Theatre, which he retained until 1800. The circus passed into the hands of Signor Corri, an Italian, who turned it into a place for concerts and other entertainments. In 1809 we find Mr. Henry Siddons in possession. He fitted it up as a Theatre, and gave performances for about two years. The building was known for some time as the Pantheon, changed in 1823 to the Royal Caledonian Theatre, and subsequently to the Adelphi Theatre. It was then used by Mr. W. H. Murray as a summer Theatre, the Shakespeare Square house, also his, being used during the winter months. It next was leased by Mr. R. H. Wyndham, but was burned in 1853. It was rebuilt and opened as the Queen's Theatre and Opera House, but was again destroyed by fire in 1865. Promptly re-erected, it was in 1875 a third time burned. After a short delay the Theatre was again reconstructed, but in the summer of 1884 it was destroyed by fire for the fourth time. The present place of entertainment is known as the Theatre Royal, and its history is one of the most chequered on record.

Excise Office, Drummond Place.

This building, which was demolished in 1846 by the Railway Company, when completing the now disused tunnel between Canal Street and Scotland Street, was for some time occupied as an office by the Board of Excise, after the previous office in St. Andrew Square had been sold to the Government. This building was formerly the town mansion of General Scott of Balcomie, the father-in-law of Mr. Canning, and was erected on the site of the mansion of Lord Provost Drummond, who had feued several acres of ground from the Governors of George Heriot's Hospital. The house stood on the east side of the present gardens in Drummond Place, and before the neighbourhood was built upon was reached by a fine avenue from the east running in the line of London Street. Mr. James Grant, in his "Old and New Edinburgh," says:—"General Scott was one of the most noted gamblers of his time. It is related of him that being one night at Stapelton's, when a messenger brought him tidings that Mrs. Scott had been delivered of a daughter, he turned laughingly to the company, and said, 'You see, gentlemen, I must be under the necessity of doubling my stakes, in order to make a fortune for this little girl.' He accordingly played rather deeper than usual, in consequence of which, after a few hours' play, he found himself a loser by £8000. This gave occasion for some of the company to rally him on his 'daughter's fortune,' but the general had an equanimity of temper that nothing could ruffle, and a judgment in play superior to most gamblers. He replied that he had still a perfect dependence on the luck of the night, and to make his words good he played steadily on, and about seven in the morning, besides clearing his £8000, he brought home £15,000. His eldest daughter, Henrietta, became Duchess of Portland."

In Drummond Place, close to this house, was the residence of Charles Kirkpatrick Sharpe, the distinguished antiquary and man of letters. He was a repository of Jacobite tradition, and his dwelling was a perfect museum, full of all kinds of curiosities; and when disposed by public auction in the rooms of Tait & Nisbet, there was a keen competition for the rich and varied assortment of treasures. Sir Walter Scott, in his Diary referring to Sharpe, says he was "a very remarkable man. He has infinite wit and a great turn for antiquarian lore. His drawings are the most fanciful and droll imaginable—a mixture between Hogarth and some of those foreign masters who painted 'Temptations of St. Anthony,' and such grotesque subjects. My idea is that Charles Kirkpatrick Sharpe, with his oddities, tastes, satire, and high aristocratic feelings, resembles Horace Walpole." Another resident in Drummond Place was Patrick Robertson, the witty Lord Robertson, traditions of whose brilliant sayings and stories form one of the glories of the Parliament House. His amplitude made him a conspicuous figure when parading the floor of the House in gown and wig. A very good story is told of Lord Robertson in connection with Sir Walter Scott. "Hush," said Robertson, one day as Scott's tall conical white head was seen advancing above the crowd in the Parliament House to the fireplace, around which stood a bevy of young advocates,—"hush, boys, here comes old Peveril, I see his Peak." "Ay, ay, my man," muttered Scott between his teeth, "as well Peveril of the Peak ony day, as Peter o' the Paunch," alluding to the portly form of the witty advocate.

The Edinburgh Academy.

BETWEEN sixty and seventy years ago a number of gentlemen, chiefly resident in the New Town, being impressed with the inconvenience of the then locality of the High School, and perhaps desiring to have their children educated apart from those of more plebeian extraction, resolved to have a new Academy, the management of which should be under their own absolute control. The requisite funds were soon provided, and the resolution carried into full effect. The building is situated on the north side of Henderson Row, overlooking the valley through which the Water of Leith flows. It was designed by Mr. William Burn, and erected in 1823, at a cost of about £12,000. Externally the Academy is a handsome structure in the Grecian style, with a fine portico, supported by six Doric columns; and its interior arrangements are, in every respect, well adapted for educational purposes. The institution is superintended by a board of fifteen directors, three of whom are elected annually from among the subscribers. Its teaching establishment includes a rector and masters, covering all the branches necessary for pupils intended for the different learned professions, the civil and military service, and mercantile pursuits. The Academy has sent forth a large number of pupils, who have achieved success and honour in different spheres of thought and action, including Dr. Campbell Tait, Archbishop of Canterbury; Sir Colin Blackburn, Professor Aytoun, the late Earl of Fife, and Mr. Grant Duff, formerly M.P. for the Elgin burghs, and subsequently Governor of Madras.

I

To the east of the Academy is the ancient village of Canonmills, in which is an old mill erected by the Canons of Holyrood Abbey for the use of their vassals in the Barony of Broughton. About 1636, the Governors of George Heriot's Hospital became proprietors of the Barony, which, added to various properties they had acquired in the district, made a considerable estate, now very valuable, from the large revenue derived from fees. Mr. Mackay, in his "History of the Barony of Broughton," says: "In the agreement made between the city and the hospital, when the mills were partly disposed of to the former, along with the superiorities of the Canongate, Pleasance, and part of Leith within the Barony, the city was taken bound, 'not to prejudice the mills, but to allow those resident in the Barony to repair to them and grind thereat, according to use and wont, and to help them to ane thirlage, so far as they can, and the same remain in their possession.' The Incorporation of the Bakers of Canongate even 'thirled' to these—that is, were compelled to have their corn ground there, or pay a certain sum." In this neighbourhood also was Canonmills Loch, drained in recent years; its site is now partly occupied by the Gymnasium and the North British Railway. On the north margin of the loch was Canonmills House, the residence of Dr. Patrick Neill, printer, who is referred to in the Chaldee MS. of *Blackwood's Magazine* as " a lean man, who hath his dwelling by the great pool to the north of the New City." On the opposite side of the Water of Leith from the Academy is Tanfield, built in 1825, as oil gasworks, but speedily abandoned. Here, in 1843, the Free Church was formally organised as a religious body, and four years later the union of the United Secession and Relief Churches as the United Presbyterian Church of Scotland took place in this hall.

Moray Place.

MORAY PLACE is a handsome street, built in the form of a pentagon, with a diameter of upwards of 900 feet. The houses are very commodious, and embrace every description of domestic requirement. The street is built on what was once a portion of the verdant and beautifully wooded park which surrounded the Earl of Moray's seat of Drumsheugh. Since their erection the houses have always been occupied by the most distinguished residents in Edinburgh. Here at one time resided Lord Jeffrey, Lord President Hope, Baron David Hume, nephew of the great historian; and Lord Moncreiff. The back windows of the houses in Moray Place overlook the picturesque ravine of the Water of Leith, and from the upper flats splendid views are obtained of the richly wooded uplands of Corstorphine and Dalmeny, combined with a long reach of the Firth of Forth, including Aberdour, Incheolm, and the finely-wooded grounds of the Earl of Moray stretching for miles along the northern shores of the Firth of Forth. Some critics, including Professor Blackie, have complained that when a stranger enters the city by the Dean Bridge, he has only presented to him a rear view of the massive buildings of Moray Place and Ainslie Place, their frontages being inward to similar structures; overlooking the fact that when this portion of the city was planned and built, the Bridge was not even contemplated.

Lord Jeffrey, while resident in an upper flat in Buccleuch Place, before his success at the bar enabled him to remove to George Street, and subsequently to Moray Place, was one of the projectors of the *Edinburgh Review*. He conducted this periodical from its establishment in 1802 until 1829, when, on being elected Dean of the Faculty of Advocates, he resigned the post in favour of Mr. Macvey Napier. He represented the city of Edinburgh in Parliament for a short time. He was appointed one of the Judges of the Court of Session in 1834, and died in Moray Place on the 26th of January 1850. A statue of him is placed in the Parliament House, and a fine monument is erected over his grave in the Dean Cemetery. Jeffrey was small in stature, which gave his friend Sydney Smith the opportunity of saying of him, "Look at my little friend Jeffrey, he hasn't body enough to cover his mind decently with, his intellect is indecently exposed." Lord Jeffrey is known in philosophy as the author of a vigorous defence of the once popular association theory of beauty, which appeared in the *Encyclopædia Britannica*. Professor Blackie, in his charming "Discourses on Beauty," after quoting some of Jeffrey's statements, says : "There must have been some extraordinary defect in the man's mind who could seriously sit down to pen such absurdities. In the same article he quotes with perfect approval, from Alison, six causes for the beauty of Greek architecture, of which symmetry is not one ! And this great multitudes of persons in metaphysical Scotland were contented to receive, for a generation, as a very sound and a very profound philosophy. How willing are men sometimes to be deluded on certain subjects and by certain instrumentalities ! And when the hour is ripe for a lie, then the more complete it is the better. Sweep the floor clean ; no matter whether you brush away dust or jewels ! Men admire thorough work." A circumstance which throws some light on Lord Jeffrey's theory of beauty is the fact that he was deficient in the sense-perception of colour.

DRAWN BY THO⁵ H. SHEPHERD.

Engraved by J. Henshall

Ainslie Place.

AINSLIE PLACE lies to the west of Moray Place, communication between the two being obtained by means of Great Stuart Street. It is in the form of a symmetrical crescent, separated by a spacious ornamental garden. The houses were built from designs supplied by Mr. Gillespie Graham. Dugald Stewart, the author of "The Philosophy of the Human Mind," was for many years a resident in this street, where he died in 1828. His widow, who survived him for ten years, was a daughter of the Hon. George Cranstoun. She occupies an honoured place among the ballad minstrels of Scotland, and her wit and talent made her very attractive. "No wonder, therefore," says a writer in the *Quarterly Review*, who evidently knew her well, "that her saloons were the resort of all that was the best of Edinburgh, the house to which strangers most eagerly sought introduction. In her Lord Dudley found indeed a friend; she was to him in the place of a mother. His respect for her was unbounded, and continued to the close. Often have we seen him, when she was stricken in years, seated near her for whole evenings, clasping her hand in both of his. Into her faithful ear he poured both his hopes and his fears, and unbosomed his inner soul; and with her he maintained a constant correspondence to the last." Dugald Stewart resided at one time in Lothian Hut, an old mansion at the east end of the Canongate, but now removed. Here he had as boarders many students of noble rank, including Henry Temple, afterwards Lord Palmerston. Dr. Robert Chambers in this connection says, "A newspaper, giving an account of Lord Palmerston's visit to Edinburgh in 1865, mentions that his lordship, during his stay in the city, was made aware that an aged woman of the name of Peggie Forbes, who had been a servant with Dugald Stewart, well remembered his lordship when under the Professor's roof in early days. Interested in the circumstance, Lord Palmerston took occasion to pay her a visit at her dwelling, No. 1 Rankeillor Street, and expressed his pleasure at renewing the acquaintance of the old domestic. Dr. John Brown had discovered the existence of this old association, and with it a box of tools which had been the property of 'Young Maister Henry.'"

In this street also resided the genial Dean Ramsay, a cadet of the Balmaine branch of the Ramsay family, and a popular dignitary of the Episcopal Church of Scotland. The memory of the Dean will long be remembered in Scotland, in virtue of his unrivalled "Reminiscences of Scottish Life and Character." About seven years ago, a memorial of Dean Ramsay was erected at the east end of St. John's Episcopal Chapel, with which he had been so long connected. It is a granite cross, 26 feet in height, with arms 8½ feet in length, ornamented with bronze bas reliefs, the whole designed by Dr. Rowand Anderson. The large panels in the base are exquisite reproductions of sculptured ornaments in Jedburgh Abbey. Another resident was George Cranstoun, Lord Corehouse, the brother of Mrs. Dugald Stewart. When a young man, his Greek scholarship secured him the friendship of Lord Monboddo, who was in the habit of saying that "Cranstoun was the only scholar in all Scotland." His lordship was the author of the clever Court of Session *jeu d'esprit* known as "The Great Diamond Beetle Case," an amusing caricature of the style of the judges in the days of our grandfathers, and the text of which is given in "Kay's Edinburgh Portraits."

The Royal Circus.

THIS Circus was designed by the late Mr. W. H. Playfair, and is built in the form of a double crescent or circle of houses, on a site which was previously occupied in part by a farm with its steading. From the great inequality of the ground on which it is erected, the southern crescent stands much higher than the northern. This, which in other circumstances might have been considered a blemish, is not so in the present instance, as it enhances the singular and picturesque grouping of the streets which lead to and look into the Circus, and harmonises well with their variety both in architecture and situation. On the south side resided for many years the late James Maidment, advocate, a friend of Sir Walter Scott's, and a distinguished peerage lawyer. Maidment was a great book-collector, and more than that, he edited and published a large number of valuable works illustrative of the political, social, and religious condition of Scotland in past times. He was the editor of an extensive collection of Scottish ballads, which is highly prized by students of that department of literature. In conjunction with his friend the late Mr. W. H. Logan, Maidment also edited a collection of the plays of the leading dramatists of the Restoration period. One of the houses in the Circus is at present occupied by the versatile Dr. Walter C. Smith, minister of the Free High Church. He is favourably known in literature as the author of several volumes of poetry, including "The Bishop's Walk," "Hilda, Among the Broken Gods;" "Borland Hall," and "North Country Folk."

In Gloucester Place, an adjoining thoroughfare, Professor

Wilson built a house, which he occupied from 1826 until his death in 1854. He was Professor of Moral Philosophy in the University of Edinburgh, and a voluminous and much-esteemed contributor to *Blackwood's Magazine*. Wilson's elaborate essay on Burns is a glowing yet critical estimate of the writings of the Scottish bard, and is perhaps the finest of the innumerable papers on the subject. Professor Wilson was the first President of the Edinburgh Philosophical Institution, in the working of which he took a lively interest.

A little way from the Circus, at the east end of India Place, is the small shop occupied by Robert Chambers as a circulating library. Here he penned "Illustrations of the Author of Waverley," a work which brought him into notice on its publication in 1822. In Doune Terrace, also in this neighbourhood, is the house occupied by Dr. Robert Chambers in his days of prosperity, and where gatherings of literary celebrities were of frequent occurrence. On the publication of the twelfth edition of "Vestiges of the Natural History of Creation" about two years ago, with an introduction by Mr. Alexander Ireland, it was announced that Dr. Robert Chambers was the author. Mr. Ireland is the last survivor of the four persons to whom the authorship was confided, and although they loyally kept the secret, it was previously very generally believed that if Robert Chambers was not the author of the book, he had something to do with it. Round the corner from the Circus, in Howe Street, there resided for some time John Ewbank, R.S.A., the gifted but unfortunate landscape painter. He was a pupil of Alexander Nasmyth, and might have attained both fame and a competency but for irregular habits, which brought him to an early grave.

St. Stephen's Church.

THIS Church, which stands at the north end of St. Vincent Street, is a massive octagonal edifice, erected in 1826-28, from a design by W. H. Playfair. The building, which cost £21,000, is in a mixed Roman style, with a handsome balustraded square tower 163 feet high. It can accommodate about 1600 worshippers, and was opened in 1828 by the Rev. Professor Brunton, husband of the author of the once popular novel " Self-Control."

Behind St. Stephen's Church are the remains of the ancient village of Silvermills. Surrounded by workshops, there are still to be found one or two of the quaint houses of the seventeenth century, with their crow-stepped gables. It is generally supposed that this village owed its origin to some of the alchemical projects of James IV. or V., both of whom were fond of making investigations, with a view to acquire supplies of the precious metals which were then supposed to abound in Scotland. Sir Archibald Napier, the father of the philosopher, was appointed Master of the Mint and superintendent of the mines and minerals within the kingdom, and it is stated on the authority of an ancient manuscript in the Cottonian Collection, that "The Laird of Merchiston got gold in Pentland Hills." The late Dr. Robert Chambers, in the last edition of his " Traditions of Edinburgh," referring to this village, says : " In 1607, silver was found in considerable abundance at Hilderstone in Linlithgowshire, on the property of the Earl of Haddington. Thirty-eight barrels of ore were sent to the Mint in the Tower of London to be tried, and were found to give about twenty-four ounces of silver for every hundredweight. Expert persons were placed upon the mine, and mills were erected in the Water of Leith for the melting and fining of the ore. The Silvermills I conceive to have been a part of the abandoned plant."

In one of the houses of Silvermills were born the brother artists, Robert Scott Lauder and James Eckford Lauder. The former was an intimate associate of David Roberts, who initiated him in the mysteries of colour preparation, and encouraged young Lauder to follow the pursuit of art. R. Scott Lauder studied at London, Venice, Bologna, Florence, and Rome. On returning from the Continent he settled for some years in London. He afterwards returned to Edinburgh, and filled the post of art-instructor in the Academy of the Edinburgh Trustees. Scott Lauder's best-known works are "The Trial of Effie Deans," "Christ Teaching Humility," "Christ Walking on the Waters," and "The Bride of Lammermoor." W. B. Johnstone, another noted artist, had his den in an old house in Silvermills, now removed. Here he painted numerous historical works, and accumulated an extensive and varied collection of Scottish antiquities. Still another artist remains to be noticed, who resided at the western extremity of Silvermills—the genial James Drummond, whose numerous historical paintings, marked by accuracy of detail, harmonious grouping, and rich colour, have secured for him an honoured place amongst the brilliant band of Scottish artists. Specially deserving notice in this work is Mr. Drummond's painting of "The Porteous Mob." The mystery surrounding the ringleaders of the band who summarily hung Porteous on a dyer's pole in the Grassmarket, is emphasized by the courtly manner of one of the leaders, whom the artist represents in the act of escorting a lady to her sedan chair, the suggestion being that the leaders belonged to the upper classes.

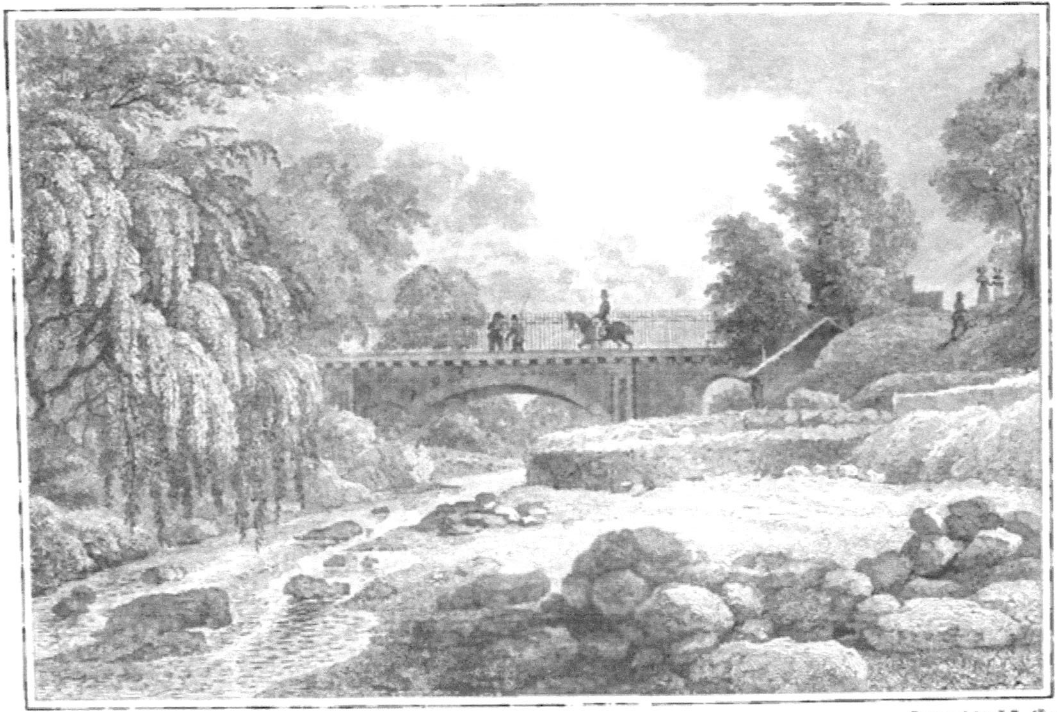

Engraved by J B Allen

Stockbridge, Water of Leith.

THE view here given is taken from a point a little below St. Bernard's Well. The Bridge represented on the engraving, and another at a short distance beyond it, connect Edinburgh proper with its north-west suburb of Stockbridge. This suburb of late years has received a great accession of elegant streets, chiefly erected on the property of the late Sir Henry Raeburn, the celebrated portrait-painter. The little "New Town" which has thus been originated, is separated from its greater neighbour by the wooded ravine through which the Water of Leith flows. In the grounds of St. Bernard's, on the spot now occupied by Ann Street, there stood, until 1825, a quaint tower erected by Walter Ross, a man of antiquarian tastes, whose residence was in the immediate vicinity. In the walls of this tower he built all the sculptured stones he could procure from old houses in Edinburgh. He possessed the four heads which adorned the old cross of Edinburgh, and when the tower was demolished they were acquired by Sir Walter Scott and removed to Abbotsford, where they may still be seen, as well as the door of the old Tolbooth of Edinburgh.

In one of the outlying streets of Stockbridge Thomas Carlyle lived for some years after his marriage, and in the same street Dr. James Browne, the author of "The History of the Highland Clans," resided for some years. Among other celebrities who have resided in Stockbridge were Sir Henry Raeburn, Professor John Wilson, David Roberts, David Scott, Thomas de Quincey, and Dr. Robert Chambers. Some deeply interesting particulars regarding the residence

of De Quincey in Stockbridge will be found in the life of
Professor Wilson, by his daughter, Mrs. Gordon, who has
supplied a graphic sketch of the idiosyncrasies of the gifted
opium-eater. With reference to his consumption of opium
Mrs. Gordon says, "An ounce of laudanum per diem pros-
trated animal life in the early part of the day. It was no
unfrequent sight to find him in his room lying upon the rug
in front of the fire, his head resting upon a book, with his
arms crossed over his breast, in profound slumber. For
several hours he would lie in this state, till the torpor passed
away. The time when he was most brilliant was generally
towards the early morning hours; and then, more than once,
in order to show him off, my father arranged his supper
parties, so that, sitting till three or four o'clock in the
morning, he brought Mr. De Quincey to that point at which,
in charm and power of conversation, he was so truly
wonderful."

Ann Street, in which many eminent individuals resided
sixty years ago, was built upon a portion of Raeburn's estate
of St. Bernard's and Deanhaugh. Writing of this street,
where Professor Wilson lived before removing to Gloucester
Place, Mrs. Gordon says, "This little street, which forms the
culminating point of the suburb of Stockbridge, was at that
time quite *out of town*, and is still a secluded place, over-
shadowed by the tall houses of Eton Terrace and Clarendon
Crescent. In withdrawing from the more fashionable part
of Edinburgh, they did not, however, exclude themselves
from the pleasures of social intercourse with the world. In
Ann Street they found a pleasant community that made
residence there far from distasteful. This street is named
after Anne, the wife of Sir Henry Raeburn, and it connects
the memory of the great painter with the locality.

St. Bernard's Well.

THIS is a circular structure, in the form of an open temple, supported by ten pillars, over a now mutilated statue of Hygeia, the goddess of health. It was erected by Lord Gardenstone in 1790, from a design by Mr. Alexander Nasmyth, artist, in grateful remembrance of the benefit received by the former from drinking of the mineral spring which it encloses. The water of the spring closely resembles that of the Harrogate wells, and is said to be of excellent medicinal quality. Its virtue, however, does not now attract so many worshippers to the temple as it was wont to do. In 1764, before the erection of the temple, one of the Edinburgh papers records that, "As many people have got benefit from using of the water of St. Bernard's Well in the neighbourhood of this city, there has been such demand for lodgings this season that there is not so much as one room to be had either at the Water of Leith or its neighbourhood." The well overhangs the Water of Leith, and has its foundation in the very bed of the river. The situation is romantic; and when the river is full, and sweeping over the shelving rocks, which here give it a noisy welcome, the scene is much admired. Last year the well and its surroundings were acquired by Mr. William Nelson, the eminent publisher, who has generously donated them to his native city.

A little to the west of St. Bernard's Well is a small irregular building, erected in 1810 over another mineral spring. The water of this well is said to have the same properties as that of the Gardenstone spring, but it has not been used for many years. The house surmounting the Well

was at one time used as a dwelling-house. Not far from
the mineral springs there resided a curious old man, who
was supported by the family of Sir Henry Raeburn, by
name Barclay, *alias* Shelley, so called, not from the poet, but
from his *shelling* the peas used in Raeburn's kitchen. This
old creature was half-witted, and used to sweep the withered
leaves from the lawn, feed and clean the pigs, &c. He was
short of stature, and of a most miserable aspect. He wore
an old grey cap crushed down on his head, and with a
grizzly beard, he was by no means attractive. He exercised
a great influence over children, and delighted to tell them
stories. He often said, as he turned round and pointed to
the river, with the long stick he always carried, " Ou ay,
bairns, I can weel remember Adam and Eve skelpin' aboot
naket amang the gowans on the braes there."

On an eminence opposite St. Bernard's Well, Walter
Ross of Deanhaugh set up a rough block of stone roughly
cut in the form of a man, which had been ordered by the
Town Council of Edinburgh in 1659 for a statue of Oliver
Cromwell. Simultaneously with the arrival of the block at
Leith, the death of the Protector was announced, and it lay
on the sands of Leith for upwards of a century, till Mr. Ross
had it removed. Dr. Wilson says, "The block was about
eight feet high, intended apparently for the upper half of the
figure. The workmen of the quarry had prepared it for the
chisel of the statuary, by giving it with the hammer the
shape of a monstrous mummy. And there stood the Protector frowning upon the city, until the death of Mr. Ross,
when it was cast down, and lay neglected for many years.
About 1825 it was again erected upon a pedestal, near the
place where it formerly stood, but it was again cast down,
and broken up for building purposes."

Engraved by W. Watkins

John Watson's Hospital.

This institution originated in a bequest, in 1759, by John Watson, writer to the signet, of the reversion of his fortune, for the endowment of a foundling hospital. Under the management of his trustees, the reversion had accumulated by 1823 to £90,000. An Act of Parliament was then applied for and obtained, authorising the fund to be applied in the endowment of a hospital for the maintenance and education of destitute children. The branches of education taught in the Hospital are English, writing, and arithmetic. The building, which was erected in 1825–28, was designed by Mr. Burn. It is of Grecian architecture, and is adorned with an elegant hexastyle portico, supported by Grecian Doric fluted columns.

A little to the east of the Hospital is the Dean Cemetery, which was formed in 1845 out of the pleasure-grounds of Dean House, once the residence of the Nisbet family. The old Manor-House of Dean, taken down in 1845, was a singularly fine specimen of the Early Domestic architecture of Scotland. Grant says: "Covered with dates, inscriptions, and armorial bearings, it was literally a history in stone of the proud but now extinct race to which it belonged." Some of the more characteristic sculptured stones of the old mansion are built into one of the walls of the Cemetery, where may still be seen two pieces of sculpture which adorned two of the windows of the house. On one of these a judge is represented throned, with a lamb in his arms; in his left hand he holds a pair of scales; his right hand grasps a sword; two rampant lions stand near, as if contending for the lamb, one of them placing a fore paw on the sword, the other placing a paw on the scales; beneath is a coat armorial—a shield charged with a chevron and three besants, with the initials A. M., for Anna Myrton of Gogar, wife of Sir John Nisbet of Dean, Bart. On the other pediment is a man armed with a thick pole, with a hook at the end, by which he grasps it; a goat is running towards him, as if in the act of butting, while a bear seizes it by the waist with his teeth, and another is lying dead beyond.

The Cemetery, which has recently been enlarged by the addition of a field to the north, is very tastefully laid out; and being bounded on one side by a steep and finely wooded bank overhanging the Water of Leith, it has many beauties. It is the favourite and fashionable place of sepulture in Edinburgh, and here many of her distinguished citizens have found a resting-place. Here lie the remains of Lords Jeffrey, Cockburn, Rutherford, and Murray; Professors John Wilson, Aytoun, Edward Forbes, John Goodsir, and Fleming; Sir William Allan, David Scott, Paul Chalmers, and Sam Bough, artists; William Brodie, sculptor; George Combe the phrenologist, and his wife, a daughter of the celebrated Mrs. Siddons; and Alexander Russel, editor of the *Scotsman*. One of the features of the Cemetery is a handsome obelisk erected to the memory of the soldiers of the Cameron Highlanders; and here also is a monument to the memory of Major Thomas Cauch, a brave soldier, whose valour at Badajoz is recorded in Napier's immortal narrative of the Peninsular War. The David Scott Monument, designed by his brother, W. Bell Scott, the poet-artist, is one of the most artistic monuments in this city of the dead. It is in the form of a Runic cross, covered with exquisite symbolic tracery, and with an effective bronze medallion of the painter, executed by his friend Sir John Steell.

Gillespie's Hospital.

THIS Hospital was founded by James Gillespie of Spylaw, who amassed a considerable fortune as a tobacco and snuff manufacturer, and bequeathed the whole of his property for the purpose of founding and endowing a Hospital for aged men and women, and a Free School for the instruction of one hundred poor boys in reading, writing, and arithmetic. In 1801 the governors of this Hospital were incorporated by royal charter, and in the same year the present Hospital was commenced. The style of the building is Gothic, of an oblong form, and the architect employed was Mr. Burn. It has three projections in front, and the whole of the angles are ornamented with turrets. The centre projection is elevated above the rest of the building, and the effect of the whole is very elegant. On the site of this Hospital formerly stood a very ancient castellated building called Wrychtishousis, at one time the residence of a branch of the Napier family.

James Gillespie is supposed to have been born in the village of Roslin. There appears to be no record of the time when he commenced business as a tobacconist. His shop was in the High Street, a short way to the east of the site of the Old Cross. He made a fortunate speculation in tobacco during the American War of Independence. He bought property at Spylaw, in the parish of Colinton, where he erected a mill for grinding snuff. Gillespie's mode of living was at all times of the plainest kind. "He invariably sat at the same table with his servants, indulging in familiar conversation, and entering with much spirit into their amusements. Newspapers were not so widely circu-

K

lated at that period as they are now; and on the return
of any of his domestics from the city, which one or other
of them visited daily, he listened with great attention to
the "news," and enjoyed with much zest the narration of
any jocular incident that had occurred. Paterson, in his
sketch of James Gillespie in Kay's Portraits, says: "Even
to extreme old age Mr. Gillespie continued to maintain the
industrious habits he had pursued through life. With an
old blanket around him, and a nightcap on, covered with
snuff, he attended regularly in the mill, superintending the
operations of his man Andrew." He kept a carriage, for
which the Hon. Henry Erskine facetiously suggested as a
motto—

> "Wha wad hae thocht it,
> That noses had bocht it."

The Merchant Company, as the governors of Gillespie's
Hospital, have in their possession a capital portrait of the
founder, by Sir James Fowlis of Woodhall, Bart., in which
the venerable tobacconist is represented seated on a rudely
formed chair or summer-seat in the garden of his house,
with his hands resting on his staff. In Kay's Portraits
there is a characteristic likeness of Gillespie, which has
long served to familiarise the public with the appearance of
the worthy tobacconist.

By alterations in the management, James Gillespie's
Hospital was in 1870 converted into a large educational
institution, and about 1000 children receive instruction
within its walls. The school is a great success, the education supplied being of a high order, while the fees are
very moderate. The Hospital still supports a number of
old men and women, but they are now boarded with their
friends.

146

The Merchant Maiden Hospital.

THE Merchant Maiden Hospital was founded in 1695, by
voluntary contribution, and appropriated to the maintenance
and education of the daughters of decayed merchant burgesses of Edinburgh. The chief contributor was Mrs. Mary
Erskine, who purchased the original house and garden
grounds near Bristo Port for £12,000 Scots, and who farther
enriched the institution by a legacy at her death. The old
building having become inconvenient, the present one was
erected from a design by Mr. W. Burn, on a large vacant
space of ground in the neighbourhood of the Meadows, on
the south side of the city. The foundation-stone was laid
in the beginning of the year 1816, and the whole finished at
an expense of about £12,000. The building is of Grecian
character, 180 feet long by about 60 in depth. It presents
a circular projection behind, and a four-columned portico in
front, taken from that of the Ionic temple on the Ilyssus.
The windows of the basement storey, which were formerly
partially hid by an artificial elevation of the ground in front,
are arched, and by appearing to support a massy basement
for the central portico and the lateral pilasters, relieve the
whole building, giving to it an air of lightness which would
otherwise have been incompatible with its extent. The
principal floor, besides a schoolroom 52 feet by 26, and other
two, 42 feet by 25 each, contains a chapel and a spacious
business room.

In 1870, owing to important changes in the administration of the educational hospitals under the management of
the Merchant Company of Edinburgh, the Merchant Maiden

Hospital was converted into George Watson's College Schools, in place of George Watson's Hospital, the Maiden Hospital being at the same time converted into a great public school for young ladies in other localities of the city, one branch being opened at the west end of Queen Street, and another in George Square. The Watson's College School was enlarged in 1872-3 by a large addition to the north front, in the shape of a lecture theatre 83 feet long, 51 feet wide, and 42 feet high. The education is of a high class, and the fees being low, the attendance is very large, the roll containing the names of over 1000 boys.

The youths attending this and the other schools of the Merchant Company are eligible for the following:—1. A presentation to one of the foundations of this or Stewart's Hospital, tenable for ten years. 2. A bursary, on leaving the schools, of £25 yearly for four years.

To the west of the Watson's College Schools is the Chalmers' Hospital, a large commodious building erected in 1861-64 by the trustees of George Chalmers, plumber, Edinburgh, who bequeathed about £30,000 for the erection and endowment of an " Hospital for the Sick and Hurt." The Hospital treats annually about 180 in-door and over 2500 out-door patients. In this neighbourhood are also the Royal Infirmary, the Edinburgh Royal Maternity and Simpson Memorial Hospital, the Sick Children's Hospital, and the Catholic Convent of St. Catherine of Sienna. The Infirmary is constructed on the pavilion or cottage system, and at present can accommodate about 600 patients in the different departments. The designs were supplied by the late David Bryce, R.S.A., and it is considered to be a very fine adaptation of the old Scottish baronial style of architecture.

Merchiston Tower.

On the outskirts of Edinburgh, close to the road to Colinton, stands the ancient seat of the Napiers, a lofty baronial fortalice surmounted by corbelled battlements and tall chimneys, evidently a structure of the fourteenth century, and scarcely altered by the ruthless hand of the modern improver. Merchiston has a special interest from having been the residence of John Napier, Baron of Merchiston, the celebrated inventor of logarithms, which he published in 1614. Napier was also the author of an ingenious exposition of the book of the Apocalypse, and this being of a speculative character, naturally attracted much attention in the seventeenth century. The Castle being in the neighbourhood of one of the principal roads to the city from the south, it is recorded that it frequently had to withstand sieges during the fierce party conflicts in Scotland. In 1571 Sir William Kirkaldy of Grange, in the interest of Queen Mary, bombarded the Castle, on the ground that certain soldiers of the King occupied it, and cut off the supply of provisions to the Castle. This unique edifice, which belongs to Lord Napier and Ettrick, is at present occupied as a private high-class academy. Within the Castle is still pointed out the little room where Logarithm Napier pursued his solitary studies, which made the common people of his day believe that he was endowed with supernatural power.

To the south-west of Merchiston Castle is the quaint mansion of Craig House, four storeys in height, with crow-stepped gables. Above the doorway are the initials S. C. P.,

and the date 1565. This house has changed hands frequently,
and been the scene of some memorable events. It is now
connected with Morningside Asylum for the Insane. It is
recorded that Kincaid, the owner of the mansion, in 1600,
went with a party of friends and armed retainers to the house
of Bailie Johnston in the village of the Water of Leith, and
forcibly abducted a widow and carried her to Craig House.
James VI., who happened to be in the neighbourhood at the
time, and hearing of the outrage, sent messengers to Kincaid,
threatening to burn his house if he did not send back the
widow. For this offence, Kincaid was fined 2500 merks, and
ordered to deliver his horse to the King. In recent years
the house was for some time the residence of Dr. John Hill
Burton the historian. The house is reputed to be haunted
by a spectre termed "The Green Lady." In the neighbourhood of Merchiston, to the east and south, was the Borough-
muir, now covered with substantial mansions, where James
IV. reviewed his troops, and encamped before the march to
Flodden. The Borestane, in which the royal standard was
planted, is placed on the side of a wall near Morningside
Church. Referring to this stone in his "Provincial Antiquities," Sir Walter Scott says, "The royal standard of
Scotland was fixed in a large upright stone called the Hare-
Stane, or boundary stone, at the place called the Borough-
moor-head, which still exists, though rendered less remarkable
by being built into the wall which runs along the side of the
footpath. At about a mile and a half's distance to the southward there is another stone, called the Buckstane, upon
which the proprietor of the barony of Pennycuick is bound
by his charter to place himself, and to wind three blasts of a
horn, when the King shall visit the Borough-moor."

Roslin, or Rosslyn Castle.

THE village of Roslin is about seven miles south of Edinburgh, and from its romantic scenery, its beautiful Chapel, and the massive ruins of the Castle, it has ever been a favourite excursion with tourists. The ruins of the Castle, the ancient seat of the St. Clairs, or Sinclairs, stand on a peninsulated rock, and are accessible only by a bridge. It is uncertain when this Castle was built. About the year 1100 William de St. Clair, son of Waldernus Compte de Clair, who came to England with William the Conqueror, obtained from Malcolm Canmore the lands and barony of Roslin. It is probable that the Castle may have been built about this time. In history little or no mention of this Castle occurs till the year 1455, when Sir James Hamilton was confined in it by James II. for taking part in the Douglas rebellion. It was burnt down in 1544 by the English forces under the Earl of Hertford. In 1650 it was battered and pillaged by troops of Cromwell under the command of General Monk. The modern part of the Castle was built in 1563, and repaired in 1622. The other parts of the Castle present only a ruin of great magnitude, large masses of the walls, which are of immense thickness, having here and there fallen down. The access to the Castle is by a narrow bridge, over a deep natural ravine, the sides of which are of solid rock. At the revolution of 1688 a lawless mob from Edinburgh pillaged the Castle, and at the same time desecrated the adjoining Chapel. Slezer, in his great work on Scotland, referring to the history of the St. Clairs and their connection with the district, says : "There goes a tradition that before the death

of any of the family of Roslin this Chapel appears to be
all on fire." Out of this bald statement Sir Walter Scott
created the weird but fascinating ballad of Rosabelle in
" The Lay of the Last Minstrel : "—

> O'er Roslin all that dreary night
>   A wondrous blaze was seen to gleam ;
> 'Twas broader than the watch-fire's light,
>   And redder than the bright moonbeam.
>
> It glared on Roslin's castled rock,
>   It ruddied all the copse-wood glen ;
> 'Twas seen from Dreyden's groves of oak,
>   And seen from caverned Hawthornden.
>
> Seemed all on fire within, around,
>   Deep sacristy and altar's pale ;
> Shone every pillar foliage-bound,
>   And glimmered all the dead men's mail.
>
> Blazed battlement and pinnet high,
>   Blazed every rose-carved buttress fair—
> So still they blaze, when fate is nigh
>   The lordly line of high St. Clair.

Roslin Chapel, which was founded in 1466 by William
St. Clair, Earl of Roslin and Orkney, Grand Master of the
Masons of Scotland, was intended for a collegiate church,
and the officials consisted of a provost, six prebendaries, and
two choristers. It appears to be part of a cruciform edifice,
but the choir was the only portion completed, as the transept,
although begun, was never finished. The late Dr. James
Fergusson, in his standard work on "The History of Architecture," points out that Roslin Chapel resembles parts of
Burgos, but that it has the greatest affinity to the chapel
at Belem in Portugal. Referring to the Chapel and its
interior decorations, Mr. Billings says : " It has little pretensions to symmetry, and its squat stumpy outline is a
great contrast to the slender grace of Melrose. All the
beauties of Roslin are superinduced on the design in the
shape of mouldings and incrustations."

Ibermitage of Braib.

ABOUT a mile to the south of Morningside Station of the Suburban Railway stands the beautiful and retired mansion of The Hermitage. It is buried in a close valley between two ranges of low and irregular hills, and is surrounded with wood. The small rivulet called the Braid Burn, which rises in the Pentlands behind Bonally, meanders through the middle of the valley on its way eastwards. The path to the house from the gate is about half a mile in length, and is cut through the deep shade of a wood, which in summer in some places is almost impervious to the light. The house, though of moderate dimensions, has an elegant exterior, and some apartments have large stores of books in all departments of literature.

The house is at present occupied by Dr. John Skelton, the gifted " Shirley," and in this lovely sequestered residence he penned many of his charming essays and studies, one of the most notable of which is an elaborate " Defence of Mary Stuart." A copy of this work having been sent to the Queen at her request, the letter intimating the receipt of the volume stated: " 'The Queen desires me to write and thank you for your ' Defence of Mary Queen of Scots,' and is most happy to have it, affording as it does conclusive evidence of the innocence of poor Queen Mary of the terrible crimes so cruelly and unjustly laid to her charge." To the north of the Braid Glen is Blackford Hill, a favourite school haunt of Sir Walter Scott, but now one of the parks of Edinburgh, its purchase having been effected during the *régime* of the late Sir George Harrison. From the summit splendid views

are to be obtained of Edinburgh and the romantic scenery
of the neighbourhood, immortalised by Scott in the passage
of " Marmion " in which Lord Marmion admires the gorgeous
view presented to his enraptured gaze when he reached this
spot.

> " The wandering eye could o'er it go,
>   And mark the distant city glow
>   With gloomy splendour red ;
>   For on the smoke-wreaths, huge and slow,
>   That round her sable turrets flow,
>   The morning beams were shed,
>   And tinged them with a lustre proud,
>   Like that which streaks a thunder-cloud.
> Such dusky grandeur clothed the height,
> Where the huge castle holds its state,
>   And all the steep slope down,
> Whose ridgy back heaves to the sky,
> Piled deep and massy, close and high,
>   Mine own romantic town !
> But northward far, with purer blaze,
> On Ochil mountains fell the rays,
> And as each heathy top they kissed,
> It gleamed a purple amethyst.
> Yonder the shores of Fife you saw ;
> Here Preston Bay and Berwick Law ;
>   And, broad between them rolled,
> The gallant Firth the eye might note,
> Whose islands on its bosom float,
>   Like emeralds chased in gold."

At Braid Farm, a short distance to the south of The
Hermitage, Miss Burnett, the youngest daughter of Lord
Monboddo, died from consumption in 1790, in her 22d
year, so that when Burns saw her during his first visit to
Edinburgh, at her father's table, she would be about 18
years of age. She was a great beauty, well read in poetry,
and being gifted with grace of manner and brilliant conversa-
tional powers, she fascinated the Ayrshire bard, who lamented
her death in an elegy marked by passionate tenderness.

154'

Craigmillar Castle.

THE picturesque ruins of Craigmillar Castle are situated upon a rocky eminence about half a mile to the south of the Duddingston Station of the Suburban Railway, and about two miles from Edinburgh. At what date Craigmillar was erected there is no record, but to judge from the style of architecture, the keep was built about the early part of the fifteenth century, and the curtain walls not long afterwards. The earliest reference to the name occurs in a charter in the reign of Alexander II., in which Henry de Craigmillar conveys a certain toft of land in Craigmillar to the Monastery of Dunfermline. The portions of the Castle still remaining supply evidence to show that they were erected at different times. The great hall is a fine apartment, 36 feet in length by 22 feet in breadth, and $24\frac{1}{2}$ feet to the apex of the pointed roof, with a spacious fireplace, 11 feet in width, quite entire. The walls of this room, which are about 9 feet in thickness, are pierced by windows on the north, south, and east, all provided with stone seats, each large enough to accommodate six or seven persons. The hall has been divided into two storeys, and a close scrutiny shows that the stone corbels for supporting the beams still retain traces of having been painted. Mr. David Ross, architect, describing the main roof of the Castle, which is almost entire, says it "is very flat, and covered with overlapping stones, the understones being wrought out with a groove along the sides of the upper surface. Two rows thus wrought were laid in their sloping position, with a space between for the overlapping stones, which extended over the grooves, the object of this

being that rain blown in beneath the edges of the overlapping row would be caught in the groove, and thus run
down the carefully-formed gutter. Throughout the whole
Castle this provision on the roofs and tops of walls to guard
against water is very marked. The parapet round the roof
is brought up flush with the face of the walls, and most of
the embrasures can still be traced.

One of the features of the Castle is a small room, 7 feet
by 5, which is shown to tourists as Queen Mary's bed-room.
There is little doubt that the date, 1474, above the main
gate, refers to some repairs. The chapel of the Castle, a
roofless building, with an inside measure of 30 feet by 14 feet
9 inches, stands between the east curtain and the inside wall.
"The chapel is lighted by two square-headed windows on the
south side, the eastern one having a mullion, and a small
circular window high up in the west gable. Inside there is a
carved piscina." King James V. resided in Craigmillar during
the time the pestilence was raging in Edinburgh; but the chief
historical associations of the Castle are those which connect
it with the beautiful but unfortunate Queen Mary. There
is no doubt that Mary frequently resided there, and that
within its walls the wily Sir James Balfour drew up the
bond for the murder of Darnley, and that there the nobles
of the land signed the document binding them to commit
the deed and to support Bothwell. This document the
astute lawyer took care should be afterwards destroyed.

A row of houses a short distance from the Castle bears
the name of Little France, and here it is believed the French
servants of the Queen resided. According to local tradition
a gigantic plane tree at Little France was planted by the
Queen, and it may be remarked that it is called to this day
" Queen Mary's Tree."

Leith Harbour, from the Pier.

THE harbour of Leith was primarily the bed of the Water of Leith, at the point where its waters join the Forth. It was of course tidal, and the landing-places were simply the banks of the stream. Commodious docks, which the rapidly increasing trade of the Port of Leith had long demanded, have been constructed from time to time, in which shipping may float during any state of the tide. The first pier at Leith, which was built of wood, was destroyed in 1544. During the seventeenth century another wooden pier was erected to accommodate the trade of the port. Some time between 1720 and 1730, a stone pier in continuation of the wooden structure was carried northwards for about 100 yards, the stones for which were brought from Culross. An attempt to enlarge the harbour was made in 1753, but owing to a want of funds, little resulted from the movement. About 100 years ago various plans were proposed for the extension of the harbour accommodation, which at length induced the Magistrates and Town Council of Edinburgh to obtain an Act of Parliament in 1778, empowering them to borrow £30,000 for the purpose of constructing a basin, or wet dock, of seven acres, above the dam of the sawmills at Leith, a lock at Sheriffbrae, and a canal of communication between the lock and basin. This plan, however, was ultimately abandoned, and application was again made to Parliament, to empower the Magistrates to borrow £160,000, to construct an extensive range of docks, stretching from the North Pier of Leith to Newhaven, with an entrance at each of these places. The eastern Wet Dock, next to the

tide-harbour of Leith, was begun in 1800, and completed
in 1806; and the Middle Dock was finished about eight
years afterwards. Each of these docks is 250 yards long
and 100 in width, both amounting to an area of about
ten acres. The third dock, which was to extend towards
Newhaven, was abandoned for want of funds. The Victoria
Dock, with an area of about five acres, was opened in 1852.
A few years later a scheme was projected for constructing
two extensive docks on the sands to the east of the pier,
and these have now been completed at an immense cost.
The last of these docks was formally opened by the Duke
of Edinburgh in 1881.

It was at the Shore of Leith that Queen Mary landed
in August 1560, when she came to mount the throne of
her ancestors, and in October 1589 James VI. embarked
from this port for Norway to bring home his bride. He
returned in May of the succeeding year, and was enthu-
siastically welcomed by his subjects. At the Shore
George IV. landed on the 15th August 1822, from the
Royal George, when he came to Scotland. Sir Walter
Scott was one of the first to welcome the King, and as
a memento of the event, a silver plate with a suitable
inscription was inserted in the exact spot where he had
landed.

At Leith there are two wooden piers, respectively
3123 and 3530 feet in length, which are much used by
the citizens of Edinburgh and Leith as a promenade.
Communication between the north end of the two piers
may be had by means of a small boat which plies regularly.
At the back of the east pier, and about three-quarters of
a mile from the Old Signal House, is the Martello Tower,
a circular bomb-proof structure, built during the war with
France, at a cost of £17,000.

The Signal Tower, Leith Harbour.

At the north end of the street called "The Shore" stands the old circular Signal Tower, which is so characteristic a feature in the old views of Leith Harbour. As figured by Shepherd, it is a lofty circular structure, from which the arrival of vessels in the Firth was watched. Maitland, in his "History of Edinburgh," says it was originally a windmill for crushing rape-seed and making oil. In an old painting of Leith Harbour executed about the year 1700, and now in the Trinity House, Leith, it is carefully indicated. This painting was discovered by a member of the Corporation during a visit to Rotterdam in 1716, and brought back. It supplies an interesting view of a locality which has since its execution been extensively altered to supply dock accommodation for the numerous vessels of large tonnage which now frequent the port. In 1830 the under walls of the Signal Tower were washed away by the waves during a severe gale, and heavy repairs were thereby rendered necessary. From the Tower a fine view of the opposite coast of Fife is obtained, while nearer can easily be seen the island of Inchkeith with its revolving light for the guidance of mariners.

Describing the ancient signal tower which formerly stood near the top of the Tolbooth Wynd, Dr. Daniel Wilson says: "It is furnished with little port-holes at the top, resembling those designed for musketry in our old Border peel-towers and fortalices, but which were constructed here, we presume, for the more peaceful object of watching the owners' merchant-vessels as they entered the Firth. An unusually striking piece of sculpture, in very bold relief,

occupies a large panel over the archway leading into the
courtyard behind. It bears the date 1678, and, amongst
sundry other antique objects, the representation of a
singularly rude specimen of mechanical ingenuity. This
consists of a crane, the whole machinery of which is comprised in one large drum or broad wheel, made to revolve
like the wire chamber of a squirrel's cage, by a poor
labourer who occupies the quadruped's place, and clambers
up, Sisyphus-like, in his endless treadmill. The perspective,
with the grouping and proportions of the whole composition,
form altogether an amusing and curious sample of both the
mechanical and the fine arts of the seventeenth century."

Colonel Fergusson, in his deeply interesting work on
Henry Erskine, referring to the attractions which a walk to
Leith Pier had for the citizens of Edinburgh after the North
Bridge was opened, says: "The pier of Leith soon became
a sort of *viva alta*, where lawyers and others were wont to
congregate of an afternoon. It is the scene of one of the
best known incidents connected with Mr. Erskine and Hugo
Arnot, who seems to have been as inexhaustible a subject for
his wit as for Kay's caricature. Meeting Mr. Arnot taking
a promenade on the pier, and eating a *spalding* or dried
haddock as he went, Henry Erskine, in allusion to his
extreme tenuity of person, is reported to have said, after
salutations had been exchanged, ' I am very glad to see you,
Hugo, looking *so like your meat.*' On stormy days, when
the sea was breaking over the pier, might sometimes be seen
the strange and weird sight of the gaunt and cadaverous
Hugo on his pale horse riding through the spray at the sea-
ward end of the pier—a most perilous performance considering the slippery state of the old wooden erection, which was
not then defended by any bulwark."

Custom=House, Leith.

THIS building, which is very capacious and extensive, was erected in 1812, at a cost of £12,617, in place of an older structure in the Tolbooth Wynd. Leith is the seaport of Edinburgh, but the foreign trade of the latter can be traced with clearness no earlier than 1329, when its inhabitants bought of Logan of Restalrig the port and mills of Leith, which were confirmed to them by Robert I. in the same year: but, having neglected to acquire a right of way to open their harbour, they made little use of it until 1398, when they purchased all the paths and passages within the lands of Restalrig, with power to load and unload ships in the Water of Leith. From that time commerce appears to have increased, and various regulations were progressively made for its improvement. In 1425 it was enacted that no person should visit foreign nations as a merchant who had " not three serplaiths of wool," or possessed goods of equal value; duties were imposed upon exported cloths and salmon, and also upon English merchandise imported. At that time the merchants of Edinburgh traded chiefly to England and Flanders, but shortly afterwards they extended their traffic to Norway, Denmark, and Sweden.

Notwithstanding this increasing intercourse with foreign countries, Edinburgh manufactures were apparently much inferior to the English; for we find that in 1430 James I. procured various articles from London for his own use. In succeeding years various statutes were enacted forbidding any person to convey money out of the kingdom, and compelling every merchant to render to the King's Mint at

L.

Edinburgh a certain quantity of bullion for all goods exported. In 1437 these exports consisted of wools, woolfells, and hides, and the imports were mercery, haberdashery, and various other articles for domestic use. In 1485 the merchants of Edinburgh, jealous of the increasing prosperity of the inhabitants of Leith, who were more advantageously situated for the purpose of commerce than themselves, passed an act forbidding any tradesman of the former town to enter into partnership with an inhabitant of Leith, under a penalty of 40s. Scots and the loss of freedom for one year. From this time Edinburgh continued to improve with a slow but gradual progress, and on the annexation of Berwick to England, Leith became the chief port of Scotland. After the battle of Pinkie, in September 1549, the English found in Leith harbour thirteen ships. The accession of James VI. to the throne of England in 1603 was highly detrimental to the commercial interests of Edinburgh, as it occasioned the removal of the court, nobility, and gentry, and consequently a smaller expenditure of money and a decreased demand for luxuries. In 1656 Leith possessed, according to Tucker's report upon the settlement of the revenues of Excise and Customs in Scotland, "Some twelve or fourteen vessells, two or three whereof are of some two or three hundred tons apiece, the rest small vessells for ladeing and carryeing out salt." The incorporation of the Merchants' Company in 1681 added considerably to the number, and these again were much increased by the augmentation of trade which followed the Union in 1707. Since then the trade of Leith has greatly increased, and the total tonnage of the vessels which arrived and sailed from Leith in 1881 was 712,056.

Exchange Buildings, Leith.

THE Exchange Buildings of Leith stand towards the north end of Constitution Street, opposite Bernard Street. They were constructed at a cost of about £16,000. This structure, which is of the Grecian style, is three storeys in height, ornamented in the centre part by an Ionic portico of four columns. There is a large hall for meetings and assemblies, and a portion of the building is used as a public reading-room. Assemblies have now ceased to be held in Leith.

A little to the east of Constitution Street are the remains of the once extensive Leith Links. This locality was much frequented by the citizens of Edinburgh during the seventeenth and eighteenth centuries for the playing of golf; and the literature of the subject contains frequent references to the gatherings on the Links. Lord President Forbes was an enthusiastic golfer, and he frequently played on Leith Links when the ground was covered with snow. Thomas Matthieson of Brechin, in his poem, " The Goff," says :—

> " Great Forbes, patron of the just,
> The dread of villains, and the good man's trust,
> When spent in toils in saving human kind,
> His body recreates and unbends his mind."

In " Humphrey Clinker " Smollett, after describing the method of playing golf, says : " Of this diversion the Scots are so fond that, when the weather will permit, you may see a multitude of all ranks, from the senator of justice to the lowest tradesmen, mingled together in their shirts, and following the balls with the utmost eagerness. Among others, I was shown one particular set of golfers, the youngest of whom was turned of fourscore. They were all

gentlemen of independent fortunes, who had amused themselves with this pastime for the best part of a century without having felt the least alarm from sickness or disgust ; and
they never went to bed without having each the best part
of a gallon of claret in his belly! Such uninterrupted exercise, co-operating with the keen air from the sea, must,
without doubt, keep the appetite always on edge, and steel
the constitution against all the common attacks of dis-
temper." Cockfighting was also indulged in on Leith Links,
and Arnot, in his "History of Edinburgh," describes a pit
which was in full operation in 1702.

Near the site of the old Council House in the Coal Hill, a
squalid street in the older portion of Leith, the grandfather
of Mr. W. E. Gladstone carried on business in a shop now
removed. In Peter Williamson's " Directory for Edinburgh
and Leith, 1786-88," which may be seen in the Signet
Library, will be found the following entry :—"Thomas Glad-
stones, flour and barley merchant, Coalhill."   John Gladstone, subsequently Sir John, was born in the Coal Hill on
the 11th December 1764, and he appears to have carried on
business in Leith for some time before removing to Liverpool.
In 1843 St. Thomas' Established Church in the Sheriff Brae
was built, after designs by John Henderson, architect, at a
cost of £10,000, all contributed by Sir John Gladstone, as a
memorial of the long connection of his family with the port
of Leith.   The church has a fine Norman doorway, surmounted by a square tower and octagonal spire.   A quaint
but crowded burying-ground, formerly connected with the
old church of North Leith, is situated close to the Water of
Leith.   It has an attraction from its containing a fine monument to the memory of Robert Nicoll, the Scottish poet, who
was interred within its walls in 1837.

The Town Hall, Leith.

THE Town Hall, which is situated at the corner of Constitution and Charlotte Streets, was erected in 1827, at a cost
of £3300. The building, although very simple, has two
ornamental fronts, respectively with Ionic pillars and Doric
porch. Towards the south end of Constitution Street is the
church of South Leith, dedicated to St. Mary, which was
declared by Parliament in 1609 to be the church of the
district. The former parish church is at Restalrig. This
church of Restalrig is of great antiquity, and references to it
are to be found in charters of the thirteenth century. The
portion of the church still standing is the choir, which, says
Dr. Wilson, "is a comparatively small though very neat
specimen of decorated English Gothic. The portion of the
choir now remaining cannot date earlier than the fourteenth
century, and is much plainer than might be expected in a
church enriched by the contributions of three successive
monarchs, and the resort of so many devout pilgrims as to
excite the special indignation of one of the earliest Assemblies
of the Kirk as a monument of idolatry. An ancient crypt
or mausoleum of an octangular form and large dimensions
stands on the south side of the church. It is constructed
internally with a groined roof springing from a single pillar
in the centre, and is still more beautifully adorned externally with some venerable yews that have taken root in the
soil accumulated on its roof. Amongst those buried in the
churchyard of Restalrig are the father of Lord Brougham,
and Colonel William Rickson, the comrade of General Wolfe,
the hero of Quebec.

Reverting to the church of South Leith, it has to be remarked that it occupies the site of a previous structure, but there is no record of the date of its erection. Maitland, in his "History of Edinburgh," speaking of this church, says: "Though I cannot ascertain the time of a chapel being first built at Leith, yet it must have been before the year 1493, for then there seems to have been considerable church work carried on at Leith. Now, whether this was the foundation of the chapel, or a rebuilding or enlargement, I cannot ascertain, though I take it to be the last most probable, and that the work carried on at that time must either have been the erection of the choir at the eastern end (which was demolished by the English army in 1543), or the side buildings or aisles, which plainly appear to be additional." Towards the close of the seventeenth century a stone tower, surmounted by a conical spire of wood and metal, was erected at the end of the church, towards the Kirkgate. In 1848 the church was restored by Mr. Thomas Hamilton, architect, when a new square tower, surmounted by an open Gothic balustrade, was erected at the north-west corner. The Rev. John Logan, an associate of Michael Bruce, the author of "The Cuckoo," was for some time minister of this church, before he went to London to end his career as a pamphleteer. Logan is generally believed to have published some of Bruce's poems as his own, and he has been severely stigmatised for this heartless fraud. Logan is the author of about a dozen of the Scripture Paraphrases used in the Presbyterian Churches, and the favourite hymn—

"The hour of my departure's come."

www.ingramcontent.com/pod-product-compliance
Lightning Source LLC
Chambersburg PA
CBHW031337070726
47496CB00017B/1190